55 South Korean Recipes for Home

By: Kelly Johnson

Table of Contents

Main Courses:

- Bibimbap (Mixed Rice with Vegetables and Meat)
- Bulgogi (Grilled Marinated Beef)
- Kimchi Jjigae (Kimchi Stew)
- Japchae (Stir-Fried Glass Noodles with Vegetables and Beef)
- Dakgalbi (Spicy Grilled Chicken)
- Sundubu-jjigae (Soft Tofu Stew)
- Samgyeopsal (Grilled Pork Belly)
- Galbi-jjim (Braised Short Ribs)
- Kimchi Fried Rice
- Tteokbokki (Spicy Rice Cake)
- Haemul Pajeon (Seafood Pancake)
- Bulgogi Jeongol (Beef Hot Pot)
- Dubu Kimchi (Tofu with Stir-Fried Kimchi)
- Bossam (Boiled Pork Wraps)
- Ojingeo Bokkeum (Spicy Stir-Fried Squid)

Side Dishes:

- Jangjorim (Soy Sauce-Braised Beef)
- Hobak Jeon (Zucchini Pancakes)
- Kongnamul Muchim (Seasoned Soybean Sprouts)
- Sigeumchi Namul (Seasoned Spinach)
- Gamja Jorim (Soy-Braised Potatoes)
- Kimchi Jun (Kimchi Pancakes)
- Myulchi Bokkeum (Stir-Fried Dried Anchovies)
- Oi Muchim (Spicy Cucumber Salad)
- Gyeran Mari (Rolled Omelette)
- Gaji Namul (Eggplant Side Dish)

Soups and Stews:

- Yukgaejang (Spicy Beef Soup)
- Miyeok Guk (Seaweed Soup)

- Doenjang Jjigae (Soybean Paste Stew)
- Kimchi Udon (Kimchi and Udon Soup)
- Sundubu Jjigae (Soft Tofu Stew)
- Yukgaejang (Spicy Chicken Soup)
- Saengseon Jjigae (Fish Stew)
- Janchi Guksu (Banquet Noodles)

Rice and Noodles:

- Kimchi Bokkeumbap (Kimchi Fried Rice)
- Japchae Bap (Mixed Rice with Stir-Fried Noodles)
- Mul Naengmyeon (Cold Buckwheat Noodles)
- Bibim Guksu (Spicy Mixed Noodles)
- Kimbap (Seaweed Rice Rolls)
- Kimchi Bokkeun Udon (Stir-Fried Kimchi Udon)

Desserts and Sweets:

- Bingsu (Shaved Ice Dessert)
- Hotteok (Sweet Pancakes)
- Yakgwa (Honey Cookies)
- Chapssal Tteok (Glutinous Rice Cake)
- Patbingsu (Red Bean Shaved Ice)
- Hoddeok (Korean Sweet Pancake)
- Injeolmi (Rice Cake Coated with Soybean Flour)

Beverages:

- Makgeolli (Traditional Rice Wine)
- Soju Cocktails
- Sikhye (Sweet Rice Drink)
- Bokbunja-ju (Black Raspberry Wine)
- Omija-cha (Five-Flavor Tea)
- Yuja-cha (Citron Tea)
- Insam-cha (Ginseng Tea)
- Saenggang-cha (Ginger Tea)
- Baekseju (Herbal Rice Wine)

Main Courses:

Bibimbap (Mixed Rice with Vegetables and Meat)

Ingredients:

For the Bibimbap Base:

- 2 cups cooked short-grain rice
- 1 cup julienned carrots, sautéed
- 1 cup blanched and seasoned spinach
- 1 cup bean sprouts, blanched
- 1 cup thinly sliced shiitake mushrooms, sautéed
- 1 cup julienned cucumber
- 4 fried eggs

For the Bibimbap Sauce (Gochujang Sauce):

- 3 tablespoons gochujang (Korean red pepper paste)
- 1 tablespoon soy sauce
- 1 tablespoon sesame oil
- 1 tablespoon sugar
- 1 tablespoon rice vinegar
- 1 clove garlic, minced
- 1 teaspoon sesame seeds

For the Meat (Optional):

- 1/2 lb (225g) beef bulgogi (thinly sliced marinated beef) or any preferred protein

For Garnish (Optional):

- Sesame seeds
- Chopped green onions

Instructions:

1. Prepare the Rice:

- Cook the short-grain rice according to the package instructions. Once cooked, fluff the rice and set aside.

2. Prepare the Vegetables:

- Julienne the carrots and cucumber. Sauté the carrots and shiitake mushrooms in a bit of oil until cooked. Blanch the spinach and bean sprouts separately, then season them with a pinch of salt and sesame oil.

3. Cook the Meat (Optional):

- If using beef bulgogi or any protein of your choice, cook it in a pan until fully cooked. Set aside.

4. Fry the Eggs:

- Fry four eggs sunny-side-up or as per your preference.

5. Make the Bibimbap Sauce:

- In a bowl, mix together gochujang, soy sauce, sesame oil, sugar, rice vinegar, minced garlic, and sesame seeds. Adjust the taste according to your preference.

6. Assemble the Bibimbap:

- In individual bowls, arrange a portion of cooked rice. Place the sautéed carrots, mushrooms, blanched spinach, bean sprouts, and julienned cucumber in sections on top of the rice.
- Add the cooked meat (if using) on one side of the bowl.
- Top each bowl with a fried egg in the center.

7. Serve:

- Drizzle the Bibimbap sauce over the ingredients. Garnish with sesame seeds and chopped green onions if desired.

8. Mix and Enjoy:

- Just before eating, mix all the ingredients together to ensure the flavors are well combined. Enjoy your Bibimbap, a delicious and colorful Korean mixed rice bowl!

Bulgogi (Grilled Marinated Beef)

Ingredients:

For the Marinade:

- 1.5 lbs (700g) thinly sliced beef (ribeye or sirloin)
- 1/2 cup soy sauce
- 1/4 cup brown sugar
- 3 tablespoons mirin (or rice wine)
- 2 tablespoons sesame oil
- 1 Asian pear, peeled, cored, and pureed (or substitute with 1/2 cup unsweetened applesauce)
- 4 cloves garlic, minced
- 1 tablespoon grated ginger
- 1 tablespoon sesame seeds
- 1/4 teaspoon black pepper

For Grilling:

- Vegetable oil for brushing the grill
- Sliced green onions and sesame seeds for garnish

Instructions:

1. Prepare the Marinade:

- In a bowl, combine soy sauce, brown sugar, mirin, sesame oil, pear puree, minced garlic, grated ginger, sesame seeds, and black pepper. Mix well until the sugar is fully dissolved.

2. Marinate the Beef:

- Place the thinly sliced beef in a shallow dish or a zip-top bag. Pour the marinade over the beef, ensuring each slice is well coated. Marinate for at least 30 minutes to 2 hours in the refrigerator. For enhanced flavor, marinate overnight.

3. Preheat the Grill:

- Preheat your grill to medium-high heat. Brush the grill grates with vegetable oil to prevent sticking.

4. Grill the Bulgogi:

- Remove the marinated beef from the refrigerator and let it come to room temperature. Shake off excess marinade.
- Grill the beef slices on the preheated grill for 2-3 minutes per side or until they are cooked to your desired doneness. Be cautious not to overcook to keep the meat tender.

5. Garnish and Serve:

- Once grilled, transfer the bulgogi to a serving plate. Sprinkle sliced green onions and sesame seeds over the top for garnish.

6. Serve:

- Serve the Bulgogi with steamed rice, lettuce leaves for wraps, or make it into a bowl with your favorite grains and vegetables.

7. Enjoy:

- Bulgogi is best enjoyed immediately while it's hot and flavorful. Savor the deliciously marinated and grilled beef with the sweet and savory taste of the marinade.

Kimchi Jjigae (Kimchi Stew)

Ingredients:

- 1 cup kimchi, aged and sour preferred, chopped
- 200g pork belly or pork shoulder, thinly sliced
- 1 onion, sliced
- 1 small carrot, sliced (optional)
- 2 cloves garlic, minced
- 1 tablespoon gochugaru (Korean red pepper flakes)
- 1 tablespoon gochujang (Korean red pepper paste)
- 1 tablespoon soy sauce
- 1 teaspoon sesame oil
- 4 cups kimchi juice (from the kimchi)
- 3 cups water or low-sodium broth
- 1 block (about 300g) firm tofu, cut into cubes
- 2 green onions, chopped
- 1 teaspoon sesame seeds (for garnish)
- Salt and pepper to taste

Instructions:

1. Prep Work:

- Chop the kimchi into bite-sized pieces. Reserve the kimchi juice for later.

2. Cook Pork and Vegetables:

- In a large pot, cook the sliced pork over medium heat until it's lightly browned.
- Add minced garlic, sliced onions, and optional sliced carrots to the pot. Cook until the vegetables are softened.

3. Add Kimchi and Seasonings:

- Add the chopped kimchi to the pot and stir. Cook for a few minutes until the kimchi is heated through.

- Add gochugaru (Korean red pepper flakes), gochujang (Korean red pepper paste), soy sauce, and sesame oil. Stir well to coat the ingredients with the seasonings.

4. Pour in Liquids:

- Pour in the kimchi juice and water (or broth) into the pot. Bring the mixture to a boil.

5. Simmer:

- Reduce the heat to low and let the stew simmer for about 20-30 minutes to allow the flavors to meld.

6. Add Tofu:

- Add the cubed tofu to the stew and gently stir. Simmer for an additional 10 minutes.

7. Season and Garnish:

- Taste the stew and adjust the seasoning with salt and pepper if needed.
- Add chopped green onions and sesame seeds for garnish.

8. Serve:

- Serve Kimchi Jjigae hot with a bowl of steamed rice. Enjoy the rich and comforting flavors of this classic Korean stew!

Japchae (Stir-Fried Glass Noodles with Vegetables and Beef)

Ingredients:

For the Noodles:

- 200g Korean sweet potato starch noodles (dangmyeon)
- 2 tablespoons sesame oil
- 2 tablespoons soy sauce
- 1 tablespoon sugar
- 1 teaspoon minced garlic
- 1 tablespoon vegetable oil (for cooking)

For the Vegetables and Beef:

- 200g beef (ribeye or sirloin), thinly sliced
- 1 onion, thinly sliced
- 1 carrot, julienned
- 1 red bell pepper, julienned
- 1 spinach bunch, blanched and squeezed dry
- 2-3 shiitake mushrooms, sliced and sautéed
- 2 green onions, cut into 2-inch lengths
- Sesame seeds (for garnish)

Instructions:

1. Prepare the Noodles:

- Cook the sweet potato starch noodles according to the package instructions. Drain and rinse under cold water to prevent sticking.
- In a bowl, mix the noodles with sesame oil, soy sauce, sugar, and minced garlic. Set aside.

2. Cook the Beef:

- In a pan, heat vegetable oil over medium heat. Stir-fry the thinly sliced beef until cooked through. Set aside.

3. Stir-Fry Vegetables:

- In the same pan, stir-fry the sliced onion, julienned carrot, julienned red bell pepper, blanched spinach, and sautéed shiitake mushrooms until they are slightly softened.

4. Combine Noodles and Vegetables:

- Add the seasoned noodles to the pan with the stir-fried vegetables. Toss everything together until well combined.
- Add the cooked beef and continue to stir-fry until the ingredients are evenly distributed and heated through.

5. Garnish and Serve:

- Garnish the Japchae with green onions and sesame seeds.

6. Serve:

- Serve Japchae warm as a main dish or a side. Enjoy the delicious combination of chewy noodles, flavorful beef, and colorful vegetables!

Note: Japchae is often served at room temperature or chilled, making it a great dish for gatherings and picnics.

Dakgalbi (Spicy Grilled Chicken)

Ingredients:

For the Marinade:

- 500g boneless, skinless chicken thighs or breasts, cut into bite-sized pieces
- 1 tablespoon soy sauce
- 1 tablespoon gochugaru (Korean red pepper flakes)
- 1 tablespoon gochujang (Korean red pepper paste)
- 1 tablespoon honey or corn syrup
- 1 tablespoon mirin or rice wine
- 1 tablespoon minced garlic
- 1 teaspoon grated ginger
- 1 tablespoon sesame oil
- Salt and pepper to taste

For the Stir-Fry:

- 1 tablespoon vegetable oil
- 1 onion, thinly sliced
- 1 sweet potato, thinly sliced
- 1 carrot, julienned
- 2 cups cabbage, chopped
- 2 green onions, cut into 2-inch lengths
- 1 cup Korean rice cakes (tteok)
- Sesame seeds (for garnish)

Instructions:

1. Marinate the Chicken:

- In a bowl, combine the chicken pieces with soy sauce, gochugaru, gochujang, honey or corn syrup, mirin, minced garlic, grated ginger, sesame oil, salt, and pepper. Mix well and let it marinate for at least 30 minutes.

2. Prepare the Vegetables:

- Thinly slice the onion, sweet potato, and julienne the carrot. Chop the cabbage and cut the green onions into 2-inch lengths.

3. Cook the Vegetables:

- In a large skillet or wok, heat vegetable oil over medium-high heat. Stir-fry the sliced onion until translucent.
- Add the marinated chicken to the skillet and cook until the chicken is no longer pink.
- Add the sweet potato, carrot, cabbage, green onions, and Korean rice cakes. Continue to stir-fry until the vegetables are tender and the chicken is fully cooked.

4. Finish and Garnish:

- Adjust the seasoning if needed. Sprinkle sesame seeds over the top for garnish.

5. Serve:

- Serve Dakgalbi hot, directly from the skillet. It is often served with a side of lettuce leaves for wrapping.

6. Enjoy:

- Enjoy the spicy and flavorful Dakgalbi with a perfect balance of chicken, vegetables, and Korean spices!

Sundubu-jjigae (Soft Tofu Stew)

Ingredients:

- 1 pack (about 14 ounces) silken or soft tofu
- 150g (about 1 cup) mixed seafood (shrimp, squid, clams, etc.), cleaned
- 1/2 cup kimchi, chopped
- 1/2 cup kimchi juice
- 1/2 onion, thinly sliced
- 1 green onion, chopped
- 1 red chili pepper, sliced (optional, for garnish)
- 1 tablespoon vegetable oil
- 1 tablespoon gochugaru (Korean red pepper flakes)
- 1 tablespoon gochujang (Korean red pepper paste)
- 2 cloves garlic, minced
- 1 tablespoon soy sauce
- 1 teaspoon sesame oil
- 2 cups anchovy or vegetable broth
- Salt and pepper to taste

Instructions:

1. Prepare Ingredients:

- Cut the soft tofu into bite-sized cubes. Prepare the seafood by cleaning and cutting it into smaller pieces if needed.

2. Sauté Aromatics:

- In a pot, heat vegetable oil over medium heat. Add sliced onions, minced garlic, and gochugaru (Korean red pepper flakes). Sauté until the onions become translucent.

3. Add Kimchi and Gochujang:

- Add chopped kimchi to the pot and stir. Cook for a few minutes until the kimchi is heated through.
- Stir in gochujang (Korean red pepper paste) to the kimchi mixture.

4. Pour in Broth:

- Pour anchovy or vegetable broth into the pot. Bring the mixture to a gentle boil.

5. Add Seafood:

- Add the mixed seafood to the boiling broth. Cook until the seafood is almost done.

6. Add Tofu and Season:

- Carefully add the soft tofu cubes to the pot. Be gentle to avoid breaking the tofu.
- Season the stew with soy sauce, sesame oil, and salt and pepper to taste.

7. Finish and Garnish:

- Add kimchi juice to the stew for extra flavor. Simmer for a few more minutes until everything is well heated.
- Garnish with chopped green onions and sliced red chili peppers for some extra spice and color.

8. Serve:

- Serve Sundubu-jjigae hot in individual bowls. It is commonly enjoyed with a bowl of steamed rice.

9. Enjoy:

- Enjoy the comforting and spicy flavors of Sundubu-jjigae, a classic Korean soft tofu stew!

Samgyeopsal (Grilled Pork Belly)

Ingredients:

- 500g pork belly, thinly sliced
- Salt for seasoning
- Black pepper (optional)
- Lettuce leaves, washed and separated
- Ssamjang (Korean dipping sauce)
- Garlic cloves, peeled
- Green onions, washed and sliced
- Sesame oil (optional)
- Sesame seeds (optional)

Instructions:

1. Prepare the Pork Belly:

   - Ensure the pork belly slices are thinly cut. If they are not pre-sliced, you can ask your butcher to do so.

2. Season the Pork:

   - Sprinkle a bit of salt over each slice of pork belly. Optionally, you can add some black pepper for extra flavor.

3. Preheat the Grill:

   - Preheat a grill or a grill pan over medium-high heat. Make sure it's well-heated for a nice sear.

4. Grill the Pork:

   - Place the seasoned pork belly slices on the hot grill. Grill each side for 1-2 minutes or until they are cooked through and have a nice char.

5. Set Up the Serving Station:

- While grilling, set up a serving station with washed lettuce leaves, ssamjang (Korean dipping sauce), peeled garlic cloves, sliced green onions, sesame oil, and sesame seeds.

6. Assemble and Eat:

- Once the pork belly is grilled to perfection, take a lettuce leaf and place a slice of grilled pork on it.
- Add a dollop of ssamjang, a piece of garlic, and some green onions.
- Optionally, drizzle a bit of sesame oil and sprinkle sesame seeds.

7. Wrap and Enjoy:

- Wrap the ingredients in the lettuce leaf like a small bundle, creating a bite-sized package.
- Enjoy the delicious Samgyeopsal wrap in one go! Repeat the process until you've had your fill.

8. Sides:

- Serve Samgyeopsal with traditional Korean side dishes like kimchi, pickled radishes, and other banchan.

Note: Samgyeopsal is often enjoyed with friends and family, making it a social and delightful meal. Adjust the condiments and sides according to your preference for a personalized dining experience.

Galbi-jjim (Braised Short Ribs)

Ingredients:

- 2 lbs beef short ribs, cut into 3-inch pieces
- 1 large onion, sliced
- 3 carrots, cut into chunks
- 1 daikon radish, peeled and cut into chunks
- 4 shiitake mushrooms, sliced
- 4 cups water
- 1 cup soy sauce
- 1 cup mirin (rice wine)
- 1 cup brown sugar
- 1/2 cup honey
- 1/4 cup sesame oil
- 8 garlic cloves, minced
- 1 tablespoon ginger, grated
- 1 teaspoon black pepper
- 2 green onions, chopped (for garnish)
- Sesame seeds (for garnish)

Instructions:

1. Prepare the Short Ribs:

- Rinse the short ribs under cold water and pat them dry with paper towels.

2. Combine Marinade:

- In a bowl, mix together soy sauce, mirin, brown sugar, honey, sesame oil, minced garlic, grated ginger, and black pepper to create the marinade.

3. Marinate the Ribs:

- Place the short ribs in a large bowl or a zip-top bag. Pour the marinade over the ribs, ensuring they are fully coated. Marinate in the refrigerator for at least 4 hours or overnight for the best flavor.

4. Braise the Short Ribs:

- Preheat the oven to 325°F (163°C).
- In a large, oven-safe pot, arrange the marinated short ribs. Add sliced onions, chunks of carrots, daikon radish, and sliced shiitake mushrooms.
- Pour water over the ingredients, ensuring they are mostly submerged.

5. Cook in the Oven:

- Cover the pot with a lid and place it in the preheated oven. Braise for 2.5 to 3 hours or until the meat is tender and falling off the bone.

6. Garnish and Serve:

- Once done, remove the pot from the oven. Garnish with chopped green onions and sesame seeds.

7. Serve:

- Serve Galbi-jjim hot over steamed rice. The flavorful braising liquid can be spooned over the rice or served as a dipping sauce.

8. Enjoy:

- Enjoy the rich and savory flavors of Galbi-jjim, a classic Korean dish that showcases the delicious tenderness of braised short ribs.

Kimchi Fried Rice

Ingredients:

- 2 cups cooked rice (preferably a day old and chilled)
- 1 cup kimchi, chopped
- 1/2 cup kimchi juice (from the kimchi)
- 200g pork belly or any protein of choice, diced (optional)
- 1 carrot, finely diced
- 1/2 onion, finely diced
- 2 cloves garlic, minced
- 2 tablespoons vegetable oil
- 2 tablespoons soy sauce
- 1 tablespoon sesame oil
- 1 teaspoon sugar
- 1/4 teaspoon black pepper
- 2 green onions, chopped
- Sesame seeds (for garnish)
- Fried eggs (optional, for serving)

Instructions:

1. Prepare Ingredients:

- Ensure that the rice is cooked and chilled. Chop the kimchi, dice the pork belly (if using), finely dice the carrot and onion, and mince the garlic.

2. Cook Protein (Optional):

- In a large pan or wok, heat 1 tablespoon of vegetable oil over medium heat. Add diced pork belly or your choice of protein and cook until browned and cooked through. Remove from the pan and set aside.

3. Sauté Vegetables:

- In the same pan, add another tablespoon of vegetable oil. Sauté diced onion, carrot, and minced garlic until the vegetables are softened.

4. Add Kimchi and Rice:

- Add chopped kimchi to the pan and stir-fry for a few minutes until it's heated through.
- Add the chilled cooked rice to the pan. Break up any clumps and mix it well with the vegetables and kimchi.

5. Season the Fried Rice:

- Pour kimchi juice over the rice and vegetables. Add soy sauce, sesame oil, sugar, and black pepper. Stir well to combine.

6. Add Protein and Green Onions:

- If you cooked pork belly or any protein separately, add it back to the pan. Stir in chopped green onions.

7. Finish and Garnish:

- Taste the fried rice and adjust the seasoning if needed. Cook for a few more minutes until everything is well heated.
- Garnish with sesame seeds for added flavor and texture.

8. Serve:

- Serve Kimchi Fried Rice hot, optionally topped with a fried egg. The runny yolk adds a delicious richness to the dish.

9. Enjoy:

- Enjoy the savory and tangy flavors of Kimchi Fried Rice, a quick and satisfying dish that's perfect for using up leftover rice and kimchi!

Tteokbokki (Spicy Rice Cake)

Ingredients:

- 2 cups cylindrical rice cakes (tteok)
- 1 cup fish cakes, sliced into bite-sized pieces
- 1/2 cup Korean soup stock or anchovy broth
- 3 tablespoons gochujang (Korean red pepper paste)
- 1 tablespoon gochugaru (Korean red pepper flakes)
- 2 tablespoons soy sauce
- 2 tablespoons sugar
- 1 tablespoon sesame oil
- 2 cloves garlic, minced
- 4 cups water
- 2 hard-boiled eggs (optional, for serving)
- Roasted sesame seeds (for garnish)
- Chopped green onions (for garnish)

Instructions:

1. Prepare Rice Cakes and Fish Cakes:

- Soak the cylindrical rice cakes (tteok) in warm water for about 30 minutes to soften them. Drain and set aside.
- If using frozen fish cakes, thaw them according to the package instructions.

2. Make Anchovy Broth:

- In a pot, bring 4 cups of water to a boil. Add Korean soup stock or anchovy broth and let it simmer for 10-15 minutes. Strain and set aside the broth.

3. Prepare the Sauce:

- In a bowl, mix gochujang (Korean red pepper paste), gochugaru (Korean red pepper flakes), soy sauce, sugar, sesame oil, and minced garlic to create the spicy sauce.

4. Cook Rice Cakes and Fish Cakes:

- In a large pan or wok, pour the anchovy broth and bring it to a simmer.

- Add the soaked rice cakes and fish cakes to the simmering broth. Cook until the rice cakes become soft and the fish cakes are heated through.

5. Add Spicy Sauce:

- Pour the prepared spicy sauce over the rice cakes and fish cakes. Stir gently to coat them evenly with the sauce.

6. Simmer:

- Simmer the mixture over medium heat, stirring occasionally, until the sauce thickens and coats the rice cakes and fish cakes. This usually takes about 10-15 minutes.

7. Garnish:

- Garnish with chopped green onions and roasted sesame seeds.

8. Serve:

- Serve Tteokbokki hot, optionally garnished with sliced hard-boiled eggs for extra richness.

9. Enjoy:

- Enjoy the deliciously spicy and chewy Tteokbokki, a popular Korean street food snack!

Haemul Pajeon (Seafood Pancake)

Ingredients:

For the Batter:

- 1 cup all-purpose flour
- 1 cup rice flour
- 1 1/2 cups cold water
- 1 egg
- 1 tablespoon soy sauce
- 1 tablespoon sesame oil
- 1/2 teaspoon salt
- 1/4 teaspoon black pepper

For the Seafood and Vegetables:

- 1/2 cup squid, cleaned and sliced into rings
- 1/2 cup shrimp, peeled and deveined
- 1/2 cup small clams, cleaned
- 1 cup green onions, chopped
- 1/2 cup onion, thinly sliced
- 1/2 cup carrot, julienned
- 1/4 cup red bell pepper, thinly sliced (optional)
- Vegetable oil for frying

Dipping Sauce:

- 2 tablespoons soy sauce
- 1 tablespoon rice vinegar
- 1 teaspoon sesame oil
- 1 teaspoon sugar
- 1/2 teaspoon red pepper flakes (optional)

Instructions:

1. Prepare Seafood and Vegetables:

- Clean and prepare the squid, shrimp, clams, green onions, onion, carrot, and any other vegetables you are using.

2. Make the Batter:

- In a large mixing bowl, whisk together all-purpose flour, rice flour, cold water, egg, soy sauce, sesame oil, salt, and black pepper until you have a smooth batter.

3. Mix Seafood and Vegetables:

- Add the prepared seafood and vegetables to the batter. Mix well to ensure they are evenly coated.

4. Heat Oil:

- Heat vegetable oil in a large non-stick skillet or pan over medium-high heat.

5. Cook the Pancake:

- Pour a ladle of the batter mixture into the hot skillet, spreading it evenly to form a pancake.
- Cook for 4-5 minutes on each side, or until both sides are golden brown and the seafood is cooked through.

6. Repeat:

- Repeat the process with the remaining batter and seafood-vegetable mixture.

7. Make Dipping Sauce:

- While the pancakes are cooking, mix together soy sauce, rice vinegar, sesame oil, sugar, and red pepper flakes (if using) to create the dipping sauce.

8. Serve:

- Cut the cooked Haemul Pajeon into smaller pieces and serve hot with the dipping sauce on the side.

9. Enjoy:

- Enjoy the delicious Haemul Pajeon, a savory Korean seafood pancake with a crispy exterior and a tender, flavorful interior!

Bulgogi Jeongol (Beef Hot Pot)

Ingredients:

For Bulgogi Marinade:

- 500g thinly sliced beef (ribeye or sirloin)
- 1/2 onion, grated
- 1/4 cup soy sauce
- 2 tablespoons sugar
- 1 tablespoon mirin (rice wine)
- 1 tablespoon sesame oil
- 1 tablespoon minced garlic
- 1 teaspoon grated ginger
- 1/4 teaspoon black pepper

For Hot Pot Base:

- 4 cups beef or vegetable broth
- 2 cups water
- 1 onion, thinly sliced
- 1 carrot, thinly sliced
- 1 zucchini, thinly sliced
- 1 leek, thinly sliced
- 200g shiitake mushrooms, sliced
- 200g enoki mushrooms, bottom ends trimmed
- 1 cup tofu, cubed
- 1 cup glass noodles (optional), soaked in warm water until softened
- 2 tablespoons soy sauce
- 1 tablespoon mirin (rice wine)
- 1 tablespoon sesame oil
- Salt and pepper to taste

For Dipping Sauce:

- 2 tablespoons soy sauce
- 1 tablespoon rice vinegar
- 1 teaspoon sesame oil
- 1 teaspoon sugar

- 1 green onion, finely chopped

Instructions:

1. Prepare Bulgogi Marinade:

    - In a bowl, combine grated onion, soy sauce, sugar, mirin, sesame oil, minced garlic, grated ginger, and black pepper. Mix well.
    - Add thinly sliced beef to the marinade, ensuring each slice is coated. Marinate for at least 30 minutes.

2. Prepare Hot Pot Base:

    - In a large hot pot or a deep skillet, combine beef or vegetable broth with water.
    - Add thinly sliced onion, carrot, zucchini, leek, shiitake mushrooms, enoki mushrooms, tofu, and glass noodles (if using). Bring the mixture to a simmer.

3. Add Bulgogi:

    - Add the marinated bulgogi to the simmering hot pot base. Stir gently to incorporate the flavors.

4. Season the Hot Pot:

    - Season the hot pot with soy sauce, mirin, sesame oil, salt, and pepper. Adjust the seasoning according to your taste.

5. Cook until Ingredients are Tender:

    - Allow the hot pot to simmer until all the ingredients are tender and cooked through. This usually takes about 15-20 minutes.

6. Make Dipping Sauce:

    - While the hot pot is simmering, mix together soy sauce, rice vinegar, sesame oil, sugar, and finely chopped green onion to create the dipping sauce.

7. Serve:

- Once the hot pot is ready, serve it hot. Ladle the Bulgogi Jeongol into bowls, and serve the dipping sauce on the side.

8. Enjoy:

- Enjoy this hearty and flavorful Bulgogi Jeongol as a comforting and communal meal with family and friends!

Dubu Kimchi (Tofu with Stir-Fried Kimchi)

Ingredients:

- 1 block (about 14 ounces) firm tofu, cut into bite-sized cubes
- 1 cup kimchi, chopped
- 1/2 onion, thinly sliced
- 1 green onion, chopped
- 2 cloves garlic, minced
- 1 tablespoon soy sauce
- 1 tablespoon gochugaru (Korean red pepper flakes)
- 1 teaspoon sugar
- 1 teaspoon sesame oil
- 1 tablespoon vegetable oil
- Sesame seeds (for garnish)

Instructions:

1. Prepare Tofu:

- Cut the firm tofu into bite-sized cubes and set aside.

2. Stir-Fry Kimchi:

- In a pan or wok, heat vegetable oil over medium heat. Add minced garlic and stir for a few seconds until fragrant.
- Add chopped kimchi to the pan and stir-fry for 3-4 minutes until it's heated through and slightly caramelized.

3. Add Vegetables:

- Add thinly sliced onion to the pan and continue to stir-fry for an additional 2-3 minutes until the onion is softened.

4. Season the Dish:

- Season the kimchi and vegetables with soy sauce, gochugaru (Korean red pepper flakes), sugar, and sesame oil. Mix well to coat everything evenly.

5. Add Tofu:

- Gently add the tofu cubes to the pan, being careful not to break them. Gently toss the tofu with the kimchi mixture.

6. Simmer:

- Allow the tofu and kimchi mixture to simmer for 5-7 minutes, allowing the flavors to meld and the tofu to absorb some of the sauce.

7. Garnish:

- Garnish the Dubu Kimchi with chopped green onions and sesame seeds.

8. Serve:

- Serve Dubu Kimchi hot as a side dish or with steamed rice.

9. Enjoy:

- Enjoy the flavorful combination of tofu and stir-fried kimchi in this simple and delicious Korean dish!

Bossam (Boiled Pork Wraps)

Ingredients:

For the Pork:

- 2-3 pounds pork belly, skin-on
- 1 cup Korean radish, julienned
- 1 cup carrot, julienned
- 6-8 garlic cloves, minced
- 1 onion, quartered
- 3 green onions, cut into large pieces
- 1 thumb-sized ginger, sliced
- 1 tablespoon whole black peppercorns
- 1 tablespoon sesame oil
- 1 tablespoon soy sauce
- 1 tablespoon rice wine (mirin)
- Water for boiling

For the Dipping Sauce:

- 2 tablespoons ssamjang (Korean soybean paste)
- 1 tablespoon doenjang (Korean fermented soybean paste)
- 1 tablespoon sesame oil
- 1 tablespoon honey or sugar
- 1 tablespoon rice vinegar
- Sesame seeds for garnish

For Wrapping:

- Napa cabbage leaves or lettuce leaves
- Korean perilla leaves (optional)
- Garlic cloves, sliced
- Sliced red or green chili peppers (optional)

Instructions:

1. Prepare Pork:

- Rinse the pork belly under cold water. In a large pot, place the pork belly along with Korean radish, carrot, garlic, onion, green onions, ginger, black peppercorns, sesame oil, soy sauce, and rice wine.
- Add enough water to the pot to cover the pork and vegetables.

2. Boil Pork:

- Bring the water to a boil over high heat. Once boiling, reduce the heat to medium-low and simmer for about 1.5 to 2 hours, or until the pork is tender.
- Check the tenderness by inserting a skewer or fork into the pork. If it goes through easily, the pork is done.

3. Cool and Slice:

- Once the pork is cooked, remove it from the pot and let it cool for a bit. Slice the pork into thin pieces.

4. Prepare Dipping Sauce:

- In a small bowl, mix ssamjang, doenjang, sesame oil, honey (or sugar), and rice vinegar to create the dipping sauce. Garnish with sesame seeds.

5. Assemble Wraps:

- To eat Bossam, take a piece of Napa cabbage or lettuce leaf, add a slice of pork, a dollop of dipping sauce, and any optional ingredients like garlic slices or chili peppers.
- Wrap it up and enjoy!

6. Serve:

- Serve Bossam with additional side dishes and rice if desired.

7. Enjoy:

- Enjoy the delicious Bossam wraps with the flavorful dipping sauce and a variety of fresh and pickled vegetables!

Ojingeo Bokkeum (Spicy Stir-Fried Squid)

Ingredients:

- 1 pound fresh squid, cleaned and sliced into rings
- 1 onion, thinly sliced
- 1 carrot, julienned
- 2-3 green onions, chopped
- 3 cloves garlic, minced
- 1 tablespoon gochugaru (Korean red pepper flakes)
- 1 tablespoon soy sauce
- 1 tablespoon gochujang (Korean red pepper paste)
- 1 tablespoon sugar
- 1 tablespoon sesame oil
- 1 tablespoon vegetable oil
- Sesame seeds for garnish

Instructions:

1. Prepare Squid:

- Clean the squid by removing the head, internal organs, and cartilage. Rinse it under cold water and pat it dry. Slice the squid into rings.

2. Stir-Fry Vegetables:

- Heat vegetable oil in a wok or a large skillet over medium-high heat. Add sliced onion, julienned carrot, and minced garlic. Stir-fry for 2-3 minutes until the vegetables are slightly softened.

3. Add Squid:

- Add the sliced squid to the vegetables in the pan. Stir-fry for an additional 2-3 minutes until the squid is cooked through.

4. Make Sauce:

- In a small bowl, mix together gochugaru (Korean red pepper flakes), soy sauce, gochujang (Korean red pepper paste), sugar, and sesame oil to create the sauce.

5. Add Sauce to Stir-Fry:

- Pour the sauce over the squid and vegetables in the pan. Mix everything well to ensure the squid and vegetables are coated evenly with the spicy sauce.

6. Cook Until Glazed:

- Continue to stir-fry for another 2-3 minutes until the sauce thickens and coats the squid and vegetables, creating a slightly glazed finish.

7. Garnish and Serve:

- Garnish the Ojingeo Bokkeum with chopped green onions and sesame seeds.

8. Serve:

- Serve Ojingeo Bokkeum hot over steamed rice as a main dish or as a side dish with other Korean dishes.

9. Enjoy:

- Enjoy the spicy and flavorful Ojingeo Bokkeum with the tender squid and a perfect balance of Korean spices!

Side Dishes:

Jangjorim (Soy Sauce-Braised Beef)

Ingredients:

- 1 pound beef (brisket, flank, or any stewing cut), thinly sliced or cut into bite-sized pieces
- 1 cup soy sauce
- 1 cup water
- 1/2 cup mirin (rice wine) or Korean rice wine
- 1/4 cup sugar
- 1 onion, thinly sliced
- 5 garlic cloves, minced
- 2-3 green onions, chopped (optional)
- 1 tablespoon sesame oil (optional)
- Hard-boiled eggs (optional, for serving)

Instructions:

1. Prepare Beef:

- If the beef is not already thinly sliced, cut it into bite-sized pieces.

2. Make Braising Liquid:

- In a pot, combine soy sauce, water, mirin, and sugar. Stir well to dissolve the sugar.

3. Braise Beef:

- Add the sliced beef, sliced onion, and minced garlic to the pot with the braising liquid.
- Bring the mixture to a boil over high heat. Once boiling, reduce the heat to low and let it simmer for about 1.5 to 2 hours, or until the beef is tender and the sauce has thickened.

4. Check Consistency:

- Occasionally check the consistency of the sauce. If it thickens too quickly, you can add a bit more water.

5. Finish and Cool:

- Once the beef is tender and the sauce has thickened to your liking, remove the pot from heat. Let it cool to room temperature.

6. Optional: Add Eggs:

- If desired, you can add hard-boiled eggs to the Jangjorim. Peel the eggs and add them to the pot during the last 15-20 minutes of simmering, allowing them to absorb the flavors.

7. Garnish (Optional):

- Garnish the Jangjorim with chopped green onions and a drizzle of sesame oil if desired.

8. Serve:

- Serve Jangjorim at room temperature or chilled. It can be enjoyed as a side dish (banchan) with rice or as a topping for bibimbap.

9. Enjoy:

- Enjoy the savory and slightly sweet flavor of Jangjorim, a classic Korean dish that's perfect for adding richness to your meal!

Hobak Jeon (Zucchini Pancakes)

Ingredients:

- 2 medium-sized zucchinis
- 1 teaspoon salt
- 1/2 cup all-purpose flour
- 1/2 cup water
- 1 egg
- 2 green onions, finely chopped
- 1/4 cup chopped Korean or regular chives
- Vegetable oil for frying
- Soy sauce for dipping (optional)

Instructions:

1. Prepare Zucchinis:

- Wash the zucchinis and cut off the ends. Grate the zucchinis using a box grater or a food processor. Place the grated zucchini in a bowl.

2. Salt Zucchinis:

- Sprinkle 1 teaspoon of salt over the grated zucchini and mix well. Let it sit for about 10 minutes to allow the salt to draw out excess moisture.

3. Squeeze out Moisture:

- After 10 minutes, squeeze out the excess moisture from the zucchini using your hands or a clean kitchen towel.

4. Make Batter:

- In a mixing bowl, combine the grated zucchini, all-purpose flour, water, egg, chopped green onions, and chives. Mix until you have a smooth batter.

5. Heat Oil:

- Heat vegetable oil in a large skillet or pan over medium heat.

6. Fry Pancakes:

   - Spoon a portion of the batter into the hot skillet, spreading it out to form a pancake. Cook until the edges are golden brown, about 3-4 minutes.
   - Flip the pancake and cook the other side until it's also golden brown and cooked through.

7. Repeat:

   - Repeat the process with the remaining batter, adding more oil to the skillet as needed.

8. Drain Excess Oil:

   - Place the cooked pancakes on a paper towel to drain any excess oil.

9. Serve:

   - Serve Hobak Jeon hot as a side dish. It can be enjoyed on its own or with a dipping sauce made of soy sauce and a splash of vinegar.

10. Enjoy:

    - Enjoy these crispy and savory Zucchini Pancakes as a delightful Korean appetizer or side dish!

Kongnamul Muchim (Seasoned Soybean Sprouts)

Ingredients:

- 2 cups soybean sprouts, washed and tails removed
- 1 tablespoon soy sauce
- 1 tablespoon sesame oil
- 1 teaspoon sugar
- 1 teaspoon gochugaru (Korean red pepper flakes)
- 1 teaspoon sesame seeds
- 2 green onions, chopped
- 1 clove garlic, minced (optional)
- Salt to taste

Instructions:

1. Blanch Soybean Sprouts:

- Bring a pot of water to boil. Add soybean sprouts and blanch for about 1-2 minutes until they are just cooked but still crisp. Drain and let them cool.

2. Season Soybean Sprouts:

- In a mixing bowl, combine soy sauce, sesame oil, sugar, gochugaru, sesame seeds, green onions, and minced garlic (if using). Mix well to create the seasoning sauce.

3. Mix with Sprouts:

- Add the blanched soybean sprouts to the bowl with the seasoning sauce. Toss the sprouts until they are evenly coated with the sauce.

4. Adjust Seasoning:

- Taste the seasoned soybean sprouts and adjust the seasoning as needed. You can add a pinch of salt if desired.

5. Serve:

- Transfer the seasoned soybean sprouts to a serving dish.

6. Garnish (Optional):

- Garnish with additional sesame seeds and chopped green onions if desired.

7. Chill (Optional):

- For enhanced flavor, you can refrigerate the seasoned soybean sprouts for about 30 minutes before serving.

8. Enjoy:

- Kongnamul Muchim is ready to be enjoyed as a refreshing and flavorful side dish or banchan in Korean cuisine. It pairs well with rice and other Korean dishes.

Sigeumchi Namul (Seasoned Spinach)

Ingredients:

- 1 bunch fresh spinach
- 1 tablespoon soy sauce
- 1 tablespoon sesame oil
- 1 teaspoon sugar
- 1 teaspoon sesame seeds
- 1 clove garlic, minced (optional)
- Salt to taste

Instructions:

1. Blanch Spinach:

    - Bring a pot of water to a boil. Wash the spinach thoroughly. Add the spinach to the boiling water and blanch for about 30 seconds to 1 minute until just wilted.

2. Rinse and Drain:

    - Quickly transfer the blanched spinach to a bowl of cold water to stop the cooking process. Drain the spinach well and gently squeeze out excess water.

3. Seasoning Sauce:

    - In a mixing bowl, combine soy sauce, sesame oil, sugar, sesame seeds, and minced garlic (if using). Mix well to create the seasoning sauce.

4. Season Spinach:

    - Place the drained and squeezed spinach in the bowl with the seasoning sauce. Toss the spinach until it's evenly coated with the sauce.

5. Adjust Seasoning:

- Taste the seasoned spinach and adjust the seasoning if needed. You can add a pinch of salt if desired.

6. Serve:

- Transfer the seasoned spinach to a serving dish.

7. Garnish (Optional):

- Garnish with additional sesame seeds if desired.

8. Enjoy:

- Sigeumchi Namul is ready to be enjoyed as a delicious and nutritious side dish or banchan in Korean cuisine. Serve it with rice and other Korean dishes for a complete meal.

Gamja Jorim (Soy-Braised Potatoes)

Ingredients:

- 4 medium-sized potatoes, peeled and cut into bite-sized cubes
- 2 tablespoons soy sauce
- 1 tablespoon sugar
- 1 tablespoon honey or corn syrup
- 1 tablespoon sesame oil
- 1 cup water
- 2 cloves garlic, minced
- 1 tablespoon vegetable oil
- Sesame seeds and chopped green onions for garnish (optional)

Instructions:

1. Prepare Potatoes:

- Peel the potatoes and cut them into bite-sized cubes.

2. Preheat Pan:

- Heat vegetable oil in a pan or pot over medium heat.

3. Saute Potatoes:

- Add the potato cubes to the pan and sauté for a few minutes until they start to brown.

4. Make Braising Liquid:

- In a bowl, mix soy sauce, sugar, honey (or corn syrup), sesame oil, minced garlic, and water to create the braising liquid.

5. Braise Potatoes:

- Pour the braising liquid over the sautéed potatoes in the pan. Stir well to coat the potatoes with the sauce.

6. Simmer:

- Bring the mixture to a boil, then reduce the heat to low. Cover the pan and simmer for about 15-20 minutes, or until the potatoes are tender and the sauce has thickened.

7. Check for Doneness:

    - Check the doneness of the potatoes by inserting a fork. If it goes through easily, the potatoes are cooked.

8. Garnish (Optional):

    - Garnish with sesame seeds and chopped green onions if desired.

9. Serve:

    - Transfer Gamja Jorim to a serving dish.

10. Enjoy:

    - Gamja Jorim is ready to be enjoyed as a savory and slightly sweet side dish in Korean cuisine. Serve it with rice and other banchan for a complete meal.

Kimchi Jun (Kimchi Pancakes)

Ingredients:

- 1 cup kimchi, chopped
- 1 cup all-purpose flour
- 1 cup water
- 1 egg
- 2 tablespoons kimchi juice
- 2 tablespoons soy sauce
- 1 tablespoon sesame oil
- 1 tablespoon rice vinegar
- 2 green onions, finely chopped
- Vegetable oil for frying

Instructions:

1. Prepare Kimchi:

- Chop the kimchi into small pieces if it's not already pre-chopped.

2. Make Batter:

- In a mixing bowl, combine all-purpose flour, water, egg, kimchi juice, soy sauce, sesame oil, and rice vinegar. Mix well until you have a smooth batter.

3. Add Kimchi and Green Onions:

- Add the chopped kimchi and finely chopped green onions to the batter. Mix thoroughly to ensure an even distribution of ingredients.

4. Heat Oil:

- Heat vegetable oil in a non-stick skillet or pan over medium-high heat.

5. Fry Pancakes:

- Scoop a ladle of the kimchi batter and pour it onto the hot skillet, spreading it out to form a pancake. Repeat for as many pancakes as your skillet can accommodate.
- Cook each pancake for 2-3 minutes on each side or until they are golden brown and crispy.

6. Drain Excess Oil:

- Place the cooked kimchi pancakes on a plate lined with paper towels to drain any excess oil.

7. Serve:

- Serve Kimchi Jun hot as a delicious and savory Korean appetizer or side dish.

8. Dipping Sauce (Optional):

- Create a dipping sauce by mixing soy sauce and rice vinegar. Serve it alongside the kimchi pancakes for extra flavor.

9. Enjoy:

- Enjoy these crispy and flavorful Kimchi Jun as a delightful addition to your Korean meal!

Myulchi Bokkeum (Stir-Fried Dried Anchovies)

Ingredients:

- 1 cup dried anchovies (myulchi), head and guts removed
- 2 tablespoons soy sauce
- 1 tablespoon sugar
- 1 tablespoon mirin (rice wine) or Korean rice wine
- 1 tablespoon vegetable oil
- 1 tablespoon sesame seeds
- 1 teaspoon sesame oil
- Optional: 1-2 cloves garlic, minced
- Optional: 1 teaspoon gochugaru (Korean red pepper flakes) for a spicy version

Instructions:

1. Prepare Dried Anchovies:

- Remove the heads and guts from the dried anchovies if they are not already cleaned. Rinse them under cold water and pat them dry with a paper towel.

2. Make Sauce:

- In a bowl, mix soy sauce, sugar, and mirin to create the sauce. If you prefer a spicy version, you can add gochugaru to the sauce.

3. Stir-Fry Anchovies:

- Heat vegetable oil in a pan or wok over medium heat. Add the dried anchovies to the pan and stir-fry for 2-3 minutes until they become golden and crispy.

4. Add Sauce:

- Pour the prepared sauce over the stir-fried anchovies. Add minced garlic at this stage if you're using it. Stir well to coat the anchovies evenly with the sauce.

5. Continue Stir-Frying:

- Continue to stir-fry the anchovies in the sauce for an additional 2-3 minutes until the sauce thickens and coats the anchovies.

6. Finish with Sesame Seeds and Sesame Oil:

    - Sprinkle sesame seeds over the stir-fried anchovies and drizzle sesame oil for added flavor. Stir to combine.

7. Check for Crispiness:

    - Taste one of the anchovies to check if they are crispy enough. If not, continue stir-frying for an extra minute.

8. Serve:

    - Transfer Myulchi Bokkeum to a serving dish.

9. Enjoy:

    - Myulchi Bokkeum is ready to be enjoyed as a delicious and savory side dish or banchan in Korean cuisine. It pairs well with rice and other Korean dishes.

Oi Muchim (Spicy Cucumber Salad)

Ingredients:

- 2 large cucumbers, thinly sliced
- 1 tablespoon soy sauce
- 1 tablespoon gochugaru (Korean red pepper flakes)
- 1 tablespoon rice vinegar
- 1 tablespoon sesame oil
- 1 teaspoon sugar
- 1 teaspoon minced garlic
- 1 teaspoon sesame seeds
- 1 green onion, finely chopped (optional)
- Salt to taste

Instructions:

1. Slice Cucumbers:

- Wash the cucumbers thoroughly. Using a knife or a mandoline, thinly slice the cucumbers. You can peel them or leave the skin on, depending on your preference.

2. Salt Cucumbers:

- Sprinkle a little salt over the sliced cucumbers and let them sit for about 10-15 minutes. This helps to draw out excess moisture.

3. Drain Excess Water:

- After 10-15 minutes, gently squeeze the cucumbers to remove excess water. Pat them dry with a paper towel.

4. Make the Dressing:

- In a mixing bowl, combine soy sauce, gochugaru, rice vinegar, sesame oil, sugar, minced garlic, and sesame seeds. Mix well to create the dressing.

5. Toss Cucumbers:

    - Add the drained and dried cucumber slices to the bowl with the dressing. Toss the cucumbers until they are evenly coated with the spicy dressing.

6. Adjust Seasoning:

    - Taste the cucumber salad and adjust the seasoning if needed. You can add more salt, sugar, or gochugaru according to your preference.

7. Garnish (Optional):

    - Garnish the Oi Muchim with finely chopped green onions if desired.

8. Chill (Optional):

    - For enhanced flavor, you can refrigerate the spicy cucumber salad for about 30 minutes before serving.

9. Serve:

    - Transfer Oi Muchim to a serving dish.

10. Enjoy:

    - Enjoy the refreshing and spicy Oi Muchim as a delightful Korean side dish, perfect for complementing your meal!

Gyeran Mari (Rolled Omelette)

Ingredients:

- 4 large eggs
- 1/4 cup milk
- 1/2 teaspoon salt
- 1/4 teaspoon black pepper
- 1 tablespoon vegetable oil
- 1/4 cup finely chopped green onions (optional)
- 1/4 cup finely diced bell peppers (optional)
- 1/4 cup finely diced ham or cooked bacon (optional)
- 1/4 cup shredded cheese (optional)

Instructions:

1. Prepare Ingredients:

- If using green onions, bell peppers, ham, or bacon, finely chop or dice them. Shred the cheese if using.

2. Whisk Eggs:

- In a bowl, crack the eggs and whisk them together. Add milk, salt, and black pepper. Continue to whisk until well combined.

3. Add Optional Ingredients:

- If using green onions, bell peppers, ham, or bacon, add them to the egg mixture. Mix well.

4. Preheat Pan:

- Heat a non-stick skillet or omelette pan over medium heat. Add vegetable oil and spread it evenly across the pan.

5. Pour Egg Mixture:

- Pour the egg mixture into the pan, making sure it covers the entire bottom.

6. Roll the Omelette:

    - As the edges of the omelette begin to set, use a spatula to lift one side and gently roll it towards the opposite side. This creates the rolled omelette.

7. Push to the Edge:

    - Push the rolled omelette to one edge of the pan.

8. Oil the Empty Space:

    - If needed, add a bit more oil to the empty space in the pan.

9. Pour More Egg Mixture:

    - Pour more egg mixture into the empty space, making sure it covers the bottom of the pan.

10. Roll Again:

    - As the new layer of egg sets, roll the previously rolled omelette over the new layer. Repeat this process until all the egg mixture is used.

11. Cook Until Set:

    - Continue cooking and rolling until the entire omelette is set and cooked through.

12. Transfer and Slice:

    - Transfer the rolled omelette to a cutting board. Allow it to cool for a moment, then slice it into bite-sized pieces.

13. Serve:

    - Serve Gyeran Mari as a delicious and visually appealing side dish or snack.

14. Enjoy:

    - Enjoy the light and fluffy Gyeran Mari, which can be customized with various ingredients to suit your taste!

Gaji Namul (Eggplant Side Dish)

Ingredients:

- 2 medium-sized eggplants
- 2 tablespoons soy sauce
- 1 tablespoon sesame oil
- 1 tablespoon sesame seeds
- 1 tablespoon green onions, finely chopped (optional)
- 1 teaspoon sugar
- 1 teaspoon minced garlic
- 1 teaspoon gochugaru (Korean red pepper flakes) for a spicy version (optional)
- Salt to taste

Instructions:

1. Prepare Eggplants:

- Wash the eggplants and cut them into thin strips or slices. If the eggplants are large, you can cut them into half-moons.

2. Steam Eggplants:

- Place the eggplant slices in a steamer and steam them for about 5-7 minutes, or until they become tender. Alternatively, you can microwave them or blanch them in boiling water.

3. Drain Excess Water:

- Once the eggplants are cooked, drain any excess water by gently pressing them with a paper towel.

4. Make the Sauce:

- In a bowl, combine soy sauce, sesame oil, sugar, minced garlic, and gochugaru if you want a spicy version. Mix well to create the sauce.

5. Toss Eggplants:

    - Place the drained eggplants in a mixing bowl. Pour the sauce over the eggplants and toss gently until the eggplants are well coated with the sauce.

6. Garnish (Optional):

    - Garnish with sesame seeds and finely chopped green onions if desired.

7. Adjust Seasoning:

    - Taste the eggplant dish and adjust the seasoning by adding salt if needed.

8. Chill (Optional):

    - For enhanced flavor, you can refrigerate the Gaji Namul for about 30 minutes before serving.

9. Serve:

    - Transfer the Gaji Namul to a serving dish.

10. Enjoy:

    - Enjoy Gaji Namul as a tasty and savory Korean side dish that complements rice and other main courses!

Soups and Stews:

Yukgaejang (Spicy Beef Soup)

Ingredients:

Broth:

- 1 pound beef brisket or flank, thinly sliced
- 1/2 cup shredded fernbrake (gosari), soaked in water
- 1/2 cup soaked and sliced Korean radish (mu)
- 8 cups water
- 2 tablespoons soy sauce
- 1 tablespoon minced garlic
- 1 tablespoon sesame oil
- Salt and pepper to taste

Vegetables and Seasonings:

- 1 cup sliced leeks or green onions
- 1 cup sliced mushrooms (shiitake or oyster mushrooms)
- 1 cup shredded carrot
- 1 cup soaked and sliced bracken fern (gosari)
- 1 cup chopped Korean watercress (minari)
- 2 tablespoons gochugaru (Korean red pepper flakes)
- 1 tablespoon soy sauce
- 1 tablespoon fish sauce
- 1 tablespoon sesame oil
- Salt and pepper to taste

Instructions:

1. Prepare Fernbrake and Radish:

- Soak shredded fernbrake (gosari) in warm water for about 30 minutes until it becomes soft. Slice soaked and peeled Korean radish (mu) into thin slices.

2. Make Broth:

   - In a large pot, add thinly sliced beef brisket or flank, soaked and drained fernbrake (gosari), sliced Korean radish (mu), water, soy sauce, minced garlic, sesame oil, salt, and pepper. Bring to a boil and let it simmer for about 30-40 minutes until the meat is tender.

3. Shred Beef:

   - Take out the beef slices, shred them using forks, and set aside.

4. Add Vegetables and Seasonings:

   - Add sliced leeks or green onions, sliced mushrooms, shredded carrot, soaked and sliced bracken fern (gosari), and chopped Korean watercress (minari) to the broth.
   - Season with gochugaru (Korean red pepper flakes), soy sauce, fish sauce, sesame oil, salt, and pepper. Simmer for an additional 15-20 minutes until the vegetables are tender.

5. Add Shredded Beef:

   - Add the shredded beef back into the soup. Allow it to simmer for an additional 10 minutes to let the flavors meld.

6. Adjust Seasoning:

   - Taste the soup and adjust the seasoning according to your preference. Add more salt, soy sauce, or pepper if needed.

7. Serve:

   - Ladle the Yukgaejang into bowls and serve it hot.

8. Enjoy:

- Enjoy this hearty and spicy Yukgaejang as a comforting soup, typically served with a bowl of steamed rice.

Miyeok Guk (Seaweed Soup)

Ingredients:

- 1 cup dried miyeok (seaweed)
- 1/2 pound beef (flank or brisket), thinly sliced
- 8 cups water
- 2 tablespoons soy sauce
- 1 tablespoon sesame oil
- 1 tablespoon minced garlic
- Salt and pepper to taste
- 2 teaspoons fish sauce (optional)
- 1 cup sliced Korean radish (mu)
- 1 cup julienned carrots
- 2 eggs, beaten
- 2 green onions, chopped

Instructions:

1. Prepare Miyeok:

- Rinse the dried miyeok (seaweed) under cold water. Soak it in a large bowl of water for about 20-30 minutes until it becomes soft. Cut it into bite-sized pieces.

2. Make Broth:

- In a large pot, bring 8 cups of water to a boil. Add the thinly sliced beef and cook for a few minutes until it's no longer pink.

3. Season Broth:

- Add soy sauce, sesame oil, minced garlic, salt, and pepper to the boiling water. Optionally, add fish sauce for additional flavor.

4. Add Vegetables:

- Add sliced Korean radish (mu) and julienned carrots to the pot. Let it simmer until the vegetables become tender.

5. Add Miyeok:

- Add the soaked and cut miyeok (seaweed) to the pot. Simmer for an additional 5-7 minutes.

6. Beat Eggs:

- While stirring the soup gently, slowly pour beaten eggs into the pot. Stir continuously to create egg ribbons in the soup.

7. Adjust Seasoning:

- Taste the soup and adjust the seasoning if necessary. Add more salt or pepper according to your preference.

8. Garnish:

- Garnish the Miyeok Guk with chopped green onions.

9. Serve:

- Ladle the seaweed soup into bowls and serve hot.

10. Enjoy:

- Enjoy Miyeok Guk as a nutritious and comforting Korean soup, often served on birthdays and special occasions as it symbolizes good health and longevity. It's also commonly enjoyed as a regular dish.

Doenjang Jjigae (Soybean Paste Stew)

Ingredients:

- 1/2 cup doenjang (Korean soybean paste)
- 1/2 pound pork belly or tofu, diced
- 1 medium-sized onion, sliced
- 1 zucchini, sliced
- 1 medium-sized potato, diced
- 2 green chili peppers, sliced (optional)
- 4 cups water or anchovy stock
- 3 cloves garlic, minced
- 1 tablespoon vegetable oil
- 1 tablespoon gochugaru (Korean red pepper flakes) for a spicy version (optional)
- 1 tablespoon sesame oil
- 1 tablespoon soy sauce
- 1 teaspoon sugar
- Salt and pepper to taste
- 2 green onions, chopped (for garnish)

Instructions:

1. Prepare Ingredients:

- Dice the pork belly or tofu. Slice the onion, zucchini, and green chili peppers.

2. Saute Ingredients:

- In a pot, heat vegetable oil over medium heat. Add the diced pork belly or tofu and sauté until they start to brown.

3. Add Vegetables:

- Add sliced onion, zucchini, potato, and green chili peppers (if using). Sauté for a few minutes until the vegetables begin to soften.

4. Make Broth:

- Pour in 4 cups of water or anchovy stock into the pot. Bring it to a gentle boil.

5. Make Seasoning Mixture:

- In a bowl, mix doenjang (soybean paste) with minced garlic, gochugaru (if using), sesame oil, soy sauce, sugar, salt, and pepper. Mix well until the doenjang is fully dissolved.

6. Add Seasoning Mixture:

- Add the prepared seasoning mixture to the pot. Stir well to combine.

7. Simmer:

- Let the stew simmer for about 15-20 minutes until the vegetables are fully cooked and the flavors meld together.

8. Adjust Seasoning:

- Taste the stew and adjust the seasoning if needed. Add more salt, soy sauce, or sugar according to your preference.

9. Garnish:

- Garnish the Doenjang Jjigae with chopped green onions.

10. Serve:

- Ladle the stew into bowls and serve hot.

11. Enjoy:

- Enjoy Doenjang Jjigae as a comforting and flavorful Korean stew. It is commonly served as a side dish with steamed rice.

Kimchi Udon (Kimchi and Udon Soup)

Ingredients:

- 1 cup kimchi, chopped
- 2 packs (about 14 oz) udon noodles
- 1/2 pound thinly sliced pork belly or pork shoulder (optional)
- 1 onion, thinly sliced
- 2 cloves garlic, minced
- 1 tablespoon vegetable oil
- 4 cups chicken or vegetable broth
- 2 tablespoons soy sauce
- 1 tablespoon gochugaru (Korean red pepper flakes)
- 1 tablespoon sesame oil
- 1 tablespoon sugar
- 2 green onions, chopped (for garnish)
- Sesame seeds (for garnish)

Instructions:

1. Prepare Udon Noodles:

- Cook udon noodles according to the package instructions. Drain and set aside.

2. Saute Pork and Vegetables:

- In a large pot or deep skillet, heat vegetable oil over medium heat. If using pork, add the thinly sliced pork and sauté until browned.
- Add minced garlic and sliced onions. Cook until the onions are softened.

3. Add Kimchi:

- Add chopped kimchi to the pot. Sauté for a few minutes until the kimchi is heated through.

4. Season:

- Add soy sauce, gochugaru (Korean red pepper flakes), sesame oil, and sugar. Mix well to combine.

5. Pour Broth:

   - Pour chicken or vegetable broth into the pot. Bring the soup to a simmer.

6. Combine with Udon:

   - Add the cooked udon noodles to the pot. Stir to combine and let it simmer for a few more minutes until everything is heated through.

7. Adjust Seasoning:

   - Taste the soup and adjust the seasoning if needed. You can add more soy sauce, gochugaru, or sugar according to your preference.

8. Garnish:

   - Garnish the Kimchi Udon with chopped green onions and sesame seeds.

9. Serve:

   - Ladle the soup into bowls and serve hot.

10. Enjoy:

    - Enjoy Kimchi Udon as a hearty and flavorful soup, perfect for warming up on chilly days!

Sundubu Jjigae (Soft Tofu Stew)

Ingredients:

- 1 pack (about 14 oz) soft or silken tofu
- 1/2 cup thinly sliced pork or beef (optional)
- 1/2 cup chopped kimchi
- 1/2 cup sliced mushrooms (shiitake or oyster)
- 1/4 cup thinly sliced onions
- 1/4 cup chopped zucchini
- 1/4 cup chopped green onions
- 1 tablespoon vegetable oil
- 2 cloves garlic, minced
- 1 tablespoon gochugaru (Korean red pepper flakes)
- 1 tablespoon soy sauce
- 1 teaspoon sesame oil
- 4 cups anchovy or vegetable broth
- 1 egg (optional)
- Salt and pepper to taste

Instructions:

1. Prepare Tofu:

- Cut the soft or silken tofu into bite-sized cubes.

2. Saute Meat and Vegetables:

- In a pot, heat vegetable oil over medium heat. If using meat, add thinly sliced pork or beef and cook until browned.
- Add minced garlic, sliced onions, chopped zucchini, and sliced mushrooms. Sauté until the vegetables are slightly softened.

3. Add Kimchi and Seasonings:

- Add chopped kimchi to the pot. Stir in gochugaru (Korean red pepper flakes), soy sauce, and sesame oil. Cook for a few minutes to enhance the flavors.

4. Pour Broth:

- Pour anchovy or vegetable broth into the pot. Bring the stew to a simmer.

5. Add Tofu:

    - Carefully add the cubed tofu to the simmering stew. Be gentle to avoid breaking the tofu.

6. Mix and Simmer:

    - Gently stir the stew to combine all the ingredients. Let it simmer for about 10-15 minutes to allow the flavors to meld.

7. Optional Egg (Gyeran):

    - If desired, crack an egg into the stew and let it cook until the whites are set but the yolk is still runny.

8. Season to Taste:

    - Taste the Sundubu Jjigae and add salt and pepper as needed.

9. Garnish:

    - Garnish with chopped green onions.

10. Serve:

    - Ladle the Sundubu Jjigae into bowls and serve hot.

11. Enjoy:

    - Enjoy this comforting and spicy Soft Tofu Stew as a satisfying Korean meal, typically served with a bowl of steamed rice.

Yukgaejang (Spicy Chicken Soup)

Ingredients:

- 1 pound (about 450g) chicken (thighs or breast), shredded
- 4 cups chicken broth
- 4 cups water
- 1/2 cup gosari (fernbrake), soaked and cut into bite-sized pieces
- 1/2 cup sliced Korean radish (mu)
- 1/2 cup shredded carrots
- 1/2 cup sliced onion
- 1/2 cup sliced mushrooms (shiitake or oyster)
- 2 tablespoons vegetable oil
- 2 tablespoons gochugaru (Korean red pepper flakes)
- 1 tablespoon soy sauce
- 1 tablespoon minced garlic
- 1 teaspoon sesame oil
- Salt and pepper to taste
- 2 eggs (optional)
- Chopped green onions for garnish

Instructions:

1. Prepare Chicken:

- Cook the chicken (thighs or breast) and shred it into bite-sized pieces.

2. Make Broth:

- In a large pot, combine chicken broth and water. Bring it to a boil.

3. Add Vegetables:

- Add soaked and cut gosari (fernbrake), sliced Korean radish (mu), shredded carrots, sliced onion, and sliced mushrooms to the boiling broth.

4. Saute Vegetables:

- In a separate pan, heat vegetable oil. Add gochugaru (Korean red pepper flakes) and soy sauce. Stir for a minute to infuse the oil.

- Add minced garlic to the pan and sauté for another minute.

5. Combine and Simmer:

    - Pour the seasoned oil mixture into the boiling broth. Stir well to combine.
    - Add the shredded chicken to the pot and let the soup simmer for about 20-25 minutes until the vegetables are tender.

6. Season:

    - Season the soup with sesame oil, salt, and pepper according to your taste preferences.

7. Optional Eggs (Gyeran):

    - If desired, crack the eggs into the boiling soup and let them cook until the whites are set but the yolk is still runny.

8. Garnish:

    - Garnish the Yukgaejang with chopped green onions.

9. Serve:

    - Ladle the spicy chicken soup into bowls and serve hot.

10. Enjoy:

    - Enjoy Yukgaejang as a flavorful and spicy Korean soup, traditionally served with a bowl of steamed rice.

Saengseon Jjigae (Fish Stew)

Ingredients:

- 1 pound white fish fillets (such as cod or haddock), cut into bite-sized pieces
- 1 onion, thinly sliced
- 1 zucchini, sliced
- 1 carrot, sliced
- 4-5 shiitake mushrooms, sliced
- 2 green onions, chopped
- 1 red or green chili pepper, sliced (optional, for spice)
- 2 cloves garlic, minced
- 1 tablespoon gochugaru (Korean red pepper flakes)
- 1 tablespoon soy sauce
- 1 tablespoon fish sauce
- 1 tablespoon sesame oil
- 6 cups fish or vegetable broth
- Salt and pepper to taste

Instructions:

1. Prepare Vegetables:

- Slice the onion, zucchini, carrot, shiitake mushrooms, green onions, and chili pepper.

2. Make Broth:

- In a pot, bring fish or vegetable broth to a simmer.

3. Add Vegetables:

- Add the sliced onion, zucchini, carrot, shiitake mushrooms, green onions, and chili pepper to the simmering broth.

4. Season:

- Add minced garlic, gochugaru (Korean red pepper flakes), soy sauce, fish sauce, and sesame oil to the pot. Stir to combine.

5. Add Fish:

    - Carefully add the bite-sized fish pieces to the stew. Let it simmer until the fish is cooked through.

6. Adjust Seasoning:

    - Taste the stew and adjust the seasoning by adding salt and pepper as needed.

7. Serve:

    - Ladle the Saengseon Jjigae into bowls.

8. Garnish:

    - Garnish with additional chopped green onions if desired.

9. Enjoy:

    - Enjoy this flavorful and comforting Fish Stew, typically served with a bowl of steamed rice in Korean cuisine.

Janchi Guksu (Banquet Noodles)

Ingredients:

- 8 oz (about 230g) thin wheat noodles (somyeon or harusame)
- 6 cups chicken or vegetable broth
- 1 cup shredded cooked chicken breast (optional)
- 1 cup julienned carrots
- 1 cup thinly sliced zucchini
- 1 cup spinach, washed and trimmed
- 4 green onions, chopped
- 2 cloves garlic, minced
- 1 tablespoon soy sauce
- 1 tablespoon sesame oil
- Salt and pepper to taste
- Toasted sesame seeds for garnish (optional)

Instructions:

1. Cook Noodles:

- Cook the thin wheat noodles according to the package instructions. Drain and set aside.

2. Prepare Vegetables:

- Julienne the carrots, thinly slice the zucchini, and chop the green onions.

3. Make Broth:

- In a large pot, bring the chicken or vegetable broth to a simmer.

4. Add Vegetables:

- Add julienned carrots and sliced zucchini to the simmering broth. Let them cook until they are tender.

5. Season Broth:

- Season the broth with minced garlic, soy sauce, sesame oil, salt, and pepper. Adjust the seasoning according to your taste.

6. Add Chicken (Optional):

    - If using shredded cooked chicken, add it to the pot. Let it simmer for a few more minutes until the chicken is heated through.

7. Blanch Spinach:

    - In a separate pot of boiling water, blanch the spinach for about 1-2 minutes until wilted. Drain and rinse with cold water to stop the cooking process.

8. Assemble Bowls:

    - Divide the cooked noodles into serving bowls. Ladle the hot broth and vegetables over the noodles.

9. Garnish:

    - Garnish each bowl with blanched spinach and chopped green onions. Optionally, sprinkle toasted sesame seeds on top.

10. Serve:

    - Serve Janchi Guksu hot.

11. Enjoy:

    - Enjoy this simple and elegant Banquet Noodles, a popular Korean dish often served on special occasions and celebrations!

Rice and Noodles:

Kimchi Bokkeumbap (Kimchi Fried Rice)

Ingredients:

- 3 cups cooked and cooled rice (preferably day-old rice)
- 1 cup kimchi, chopped
- 1/2 cup kimchi juice
- 1/2 cup cooked protein (chicken, pork, beef, shrimp, or tofu), diced
- 1/2 cup carrots, finely diced
- 1/2 cup peas or other vegetables (optional)
- 2 tablespoons vegetable oil
- 2 cloves garlic, minced
- 1 tablespoon soy sauce
- 1 tablespoon gochugaru (Korean red pepper flakes)
- 1 tablespoon sesame oil
- 2 green onions, chopped
- Sesame seeds for garnish
- Fried eggs for serving (optional)

Instructions:

1. Prepare Ingredients:

- Chop the kimchi and dice the cooked protein and carrots.

2. Heat Pan:

- Heat vegetable oil in a large pan or wok over medium-high heat.

3. Saute Aromatics:

- Add minced garlic to the hot oil and sauté for about 30 seconds until fragrant.

4. Add Kimchi:

- Add chopped kimchi to the pan and stir-fry for 2-3 minutes until it's slightly caramelized.

5. Add Vegetables and Protein:

   - Add diced carrots and peas (or other vegetables) to the pan. Stir-fry for an additional 2-3 minutes until the vegetables are tender.
   - Add the diced cooked protein to the pan and stir to combine with the vegetables and kimchi.

6. Add Rice:

   - Break up the day-old rice and add it to the pan. Stir-fry, mixing well with the other ingredients.

7. Season:

   - Pour kimchi juice over the rice and add soy sauce, gochugaru (Korean red pepper flakes), and sesame oil. Mix thoroughly to ensure the rice is well coated and seasoned.

8. Add Green Onions:

   - Add chopped green onions to the pan and continue to stir-fry for another 2-3 minutes.

9. Garnish:

   - Garnish with sesame seeds for extra flavor and a touch of nuttiness.

10. Serve:

    - Serve Kimchi Bokkeumbap hot.

11. Optional:

    - Top each serving with a fried egg for an extra delicious and traditional touch.

12. Enjoy:

    - Enjoy this flavorful and satisfying Kimchi Fried Rice as a standalone dish or as a side to complement your Korean meal!

Japchae Bap (Mixed Rice with Stir-Fried Noodles)

Ingredients:

For Japchae:

- 4 oz sweet potato starch noodles (dangmyeon)
- 2 tablespoons vegetable oil, divided
- 1 cup thinly sliced beef (ribeye or sirloin)
- 1 cup julienned carrots
- 1 cup sliced shiitake mushrooms
- 1 cup spinach, washed and trimmed
- 1 cup thinly sliced bell peppers (red and yellow)
- 2 tablespoons soy sauce
- 1 tablespoon sugar
- 1 tablespoon sesame oil
- Toasted sesame seeds for garnish

For Mixed Rice:

- 3 cups cooked short-grain rice (preferably slightly cooled)
- 1 tablespoon soy sauce
- 1 tablespoon sesame oil
- 1 tablespoon chopped green onions for garnish

Instructions:

1. Prepare Sweet Potato Noodles:

- Cook sweet potato starch noodles (dangmyeon) according to the package instructions. Drain, rinse with cold water, and set aside.

2. Stir-Fry Beef:

- In a large pan or wok, heat 1 tablespoon of vegetable oil over medium-high heat. Add thinly sliced beef and stir-fry until cooked. Remove the beef from the pan and set aside.

3. Stir-Fry Vegetables:

- In the same pan, add another tablespoon of vegetable oil. Stir-fry julienned carrots, sliced shiitake mushrooms, spinach, and sliced bell peppers until they are tender.

4. Combine with Noodles:

- Add the cooked sweet potato noodles to the pan with the vegetables. Mix well.

5. Season:

- In a small bowl, mix soy sauce, sugar, and sesame oil. Pour the sauce over the noodles and vegetables. Add the cooked beef back to the pan. Stir-fry until everything is well coated and heated through.

6. Prepare Mixed Rice:

- In a separate bowl, mix cooked short-grain rice with soy sauce and sesame oil. Toss to combine.

7. Assemble Japchae Bap:

- In serving bowls or plates, arrange a portion of mixed rice and top it with a generous serving of Japchae.

8. Garnish:

- Garnish with chopped green onions and toasted sesame seeds.

9. Serve:

- Serve Japchae Bap immediately.

10. Enjoy:

- Enjoy this delicious and satisfying Korean dish that combines the savory flavors of Japchae with the comforting elements of mixed rice!

Mul Naengmyeon (Cold Buckwheat Noodles)

Ingredients:

For Broth:

- 6 cups beef broth
- 2 tablespoons soy sauce
- 1 tablespoon sugar
- 3 tablespoons rice vinegar
- 1 teaspoon salt
- 2 cloves garlic, minced
- 1 teaspoon ginger, minced
- 1/2 teaspoon black pepper

For Noodles and Toppings:

- 2 packs (about 14 oz) mul naengmyeon noodles (buckwheat noodles)
- 1 cup cucumber, julienned
- 1 cup Korean pear or apple, julienned
- 2 boiled eggs, sliced
- 1 tablespoon toasted sesame seeds
- Ice cubes (optional)

Instructions:

1. Prepare Broth:

- In a large bowl, mix beef broth, soy sauce, sugar, rice vinegar, salt, minced garlic, minced ginger, and black pepper. Stir until well combined. Place the broth in the refrigerator to chill.

2. Cook Noodles:

- Cook the mul naengmyeon noodles according to the package instructions. Once cooked, rinse the noodles under cold running water until they are cool. Drain well.

3. Assemble Noodles:

- Divide the cold noodles among serving bowls. Optionally, add a few ice cubes to each bowl to keep the noodles extra cold.

4. Pour Chilled Broth:

- Pour the chilled broth over the noodles in each bowl.

5. Add Toppings:

- Top the noodles with julienned cucumber, julienned Korean pear or apple, and sliced boiled eggs.

6. Garnish:

- Sprinkle toasted sesame seeds over the top as a garnish.

7. Serve:

- Serve Mul Naengmyeon immediately while it's cold.

8. Enjoy:

- Enjoy this refreshing and tangy Cold Buckwheat Noodles, perfect for a hot day or as a light and refreshing meal!

Bibim Guksu (Spicy Mixed Noodles)

Ingredients:

For Noodles:

- 8 oz somyeon (thin wheat noodles) or soba noodles
- 1 tablespoon sesame oil

For Sauce:

- 3 tablespoons gochujang (Korean red pepper paste)
- 2 tablespoons soy sauce
- 1 tablespoon sugar
- 1 tablespoon rice vinegar
- 1 tablespoon sesame oil
- 1 tablespoon water
- 1 clove garlic, minced
- 1 teaspoon grated ginger

For Toppings:

- 1 cucumber, julienned
- 1 carrot, julienned
- 1/2 cup mung bean sprouts, blanched
- 2 boiled eggs, sliced
- 2 tablespoons toasted sesame seeds
- 2 green onions, chopped

Instructions:

1. Cook Noodles:

- Cook the somyeon or soba noodles according to the package instructions. Drain and rinse under cold water to cool them down.

2. Mix with Sesame Oil:

- Toss the cooked and cooled noodles with 1 tablespoon of sesame oil to prevent them from sticking.

3. Prepare Sauce:

- In a bowl, mix together gochujang, soy sauce, sugar, rice vinegar, sesame oil, water, minced garlic, and grated ginger. Stir until the sugar is dissolved.

4. Assemble Bibim Guksu:

- In serving bowls, place a portion of the cooked noodles.
- Pour the spicy sauce over the noodles and toss well to coat them evenly.

5. Add Toppings:

- Top the noodles with julienned cucumber, julienned carrot, blanched mung bean sprouts, sliced boiled eggs, toasted sesame seeds, and chopped green onions.

6. Mix and Serve:

- Mix all the ingredients together, ensuring that the sauce and toppings are well distributed.

7. Enjoy:

- Enjoy this flavorful and spicy Bibim Guksu as a refreshing and satisfying Korean dish, perfect for a quick and delicious meal!

Kimbap (Seaweed Rice Rolls)

Ingredients:

For Rice:

- 3 cups cooked short-grain rice
- 2 tablespoons rice vinegar
- 1 tablespoon sugar
- 1 teaspoon salt

For Filling:

- 5 sheets of roasted seaweed (nori)
- 1 carrot, julienned
- 1 cucumber, julienned
- 5 imitation crab sticks or cooked ham, sliced into thin strips
- 5 strips yellow pickled radish (danmuji)
- 5 slices of cooked egg omelet
- Sesame oil (for brushing)

Dipping Sauce (Optional):

- Soy sauce
- Wasabi
- Sesame oil

Instructions:

1. Prepare Rice:

- In a bowl, mix cooked short-grain rice with rice vinegar, sugar, and salt. Allow the rice to cool to room temperature.

2. Prepare Ingredients:

- Julienne the carrot and cucumber. Slice the imitation crab sticks or cooked ham, yellow pickled radish (danmuji), and cooked egg omelet into thin strips.

3. Place Seaweed Sheets:

- Lay a bamboo sushi rolling mat on a clean surface. Place a sheet of roasted seaweed (nori) shiny side down on the mat.

4. Spread Rice:

    - Wet your fingers with water to prevent the rice from sticking. Spread a thin layer of rice evenly over the seaweed, leaving about 1 inch of seaweed on the top edge.

5. Arrange Filling:

    - Arrange the julienned carrot, cucumber, crab sticks or ham, yellow pickled radish, and egg omelet strips horizontally on the lower half of the rice.

6. Roll Kimbap:

    - Lift the bamboo mat's bottom edge with your thumbs, and fold it over the filling. Continue to roll, applying gentle pressure, until you reach the top edge. Wet the exposed seaweed edge with a little water to seal the roll.

7. Slice and Repeat:

    - Using a sharp knife, slice the rolled kimbap into bite-sized pieces. Repeat the process with the remaining ingredients.

8. Brush with Sesame Oil:

    - Brush the outer surface of the kimbap rolls with a little sesame oil for a shiny appearance.

9. Serve and Enjoy:

    - Arrange the sliced kimbap on a plate and serve with soy sauce for dipping. Optionally, mix soy sauce with a little wasabi and sesame oil for extra flavor.

10. Enjoy:

    - Enjoy these delicious and portable seaweed rice rolls as a light and flavorful snack or meal!

Kimchi Bokkeun Udon (Stir-Fried Kimchi Udon)

Ingredients:

- 2 packs (about 14 oz) udon noodles
- 1 cup kimchi, chopped
- 1/2 cup kimchi juice
- 1/2 cup thinly sliced pork belly or pork shoulder (optional)
- 1/2 cup sliced shiitake mushrooms
- 1/4 cup soy sauce
- 2 tablespoons gochugaru (Korean red pepper flakes)
- 1 tablespoon sugar
- 1 tablespoon sesame oil
- 1 tablespoon vegetable oil
- 2 cloves garlic, minced
- 1 teaspoon grated ginger
- 2 green onions, chopped
- Sesame seeds for garnish

Instructions:

1. Cook Udon Noodles:

- Cook the udon noodles according to the package instructions. Drain and set aside.

2. Stir-Fry Pork (Optional):

- If using pork, heat vegetable oil in a large pan or wok over medium-high heat. Add thinly sliced pork and cook until browned. Remove excess oil if needed.

3. Add Aromatics:

- Add minced garlic and grated ginger to the pan. Sauté for about 30 seconds until fragrant.

4. Add Kimchi:

- Add chopped kimchi to the pan. Stir-fry for 2-3 minutes until the kimchi is heated through.

5. Add Mushrooms:

    - Add sliced shiitake mushrooms to the pan. Cook until the mushrooms are softened.

6. Mix Sauce:

    - In a bowl, mix kimchi juice, soy sauce, gochugaru (Korean red pepper flakes), sugar, and sesame oil.

7. Stir-Fry Udon:

    - Add the cooked udon noodles to the pan. Pour the sauce over the noodles and stir-fry to combine everything evenly.

8. Finish and Garnish:

    - Add green onions to the pan and continue to stir-fry for another 1-2 minutes.
    - Garnish with sesame seeds for added flavor and texture.

9. Serve:

    - Serve Kimchi Bokkeun Udon hot.

10. Enjoy:

    - Enjoy this spicy and savory Stir-Fried Kimchi Udon as a delicious and comforting Korean dish!

Desserts and Sweets:

Bingsu (Shaved Ice Dessert)

Ingredients:

For Shaved Ice:

- 4 cups shaved ice or finely crushed ice

For Red Bean Topping:

- 1 cup sweetened red bean paste (pat or adzuki bean paste)

For Milk Drizzle:

- 1/2 cup condensed milk or sweetened condensed milk

For Toppings (Optional):

- Fresh fruit slices (strawberries, mango, kiwi)
- Rice cakes (tteok)
- Nuts (almonds, peanuts)
- Cereal flakes
- Ice cream (vanilla, green tea, or other flavors)

Instructions:

1. Prepare Shaved Ice:

- If you don't have a shaved ice machine, you can crush ice in a blender until it reaches a snow-like consistency. Alternatively, you can buy pre-shaved ice.

2. Assemble Bingsu:

- Place the shaved ice in a large bowl or serving dish.

3. Add Red Bean Topping:

- Spoon sweetened red bean paste over the shaved ice. You can adjust the amount according to your preference.

4. Drizzle with Milk:

- Generously drizzle condensed milk or sweetened condensed milk over the shaved ice and red bean paste. The amount can be adjusted based on your sweetness preference.

5. Add Toppings:

- Customize your bingsu with various toppings. Add fresh fruit slices, rice cakes, nuts, cereal flakes, or a scoop of ice cream.

6. Serve Immediately:

- Bingsu is best enjoyed immediately before the shaved ice begins to melt.

7. Enjoy:

- Indulge in the refreshing and sweet flavors of Bingsu, a popular Korean shaved ice dessert, especially delightful on a hot day!

Hotteok (Sweet Pancakes)

Ingredients:

For Dough:

- 2 cups all-purpose flour
- 1 cup lukewarm water
- 1 teaspoon active dry yeast
- 1 tablespoon sugar
- 1/4 teaspoon salt

For Filling:

- 1/2 cup brown sugar
- 1/2 cup chopped nuts (peanuts, walnuts, or a mix)
- 1 teaspoon ground cinnamon

For Cooking:

- Vegetable oil for pan-frying

Instructions:

1. Activate Yeast:

- In a bowl, combine lukewarm water, sugar, and active dry yeast. Let it sit for about 5-10 minutes until the mixture becomes frothy.

2. Make Dough:

- In a large mixing bowl, combine the flour, salt, and the activated yeast mixture. Mix well until a sticky dough forms.
- Cover the bowl with a clean kitchen towel and let the dough rise in a warm place for 1-2 hours until it doubles in size.

3. Prepare Filling:

- In a separate bowl, mix brown sugar, chopped nuts, and ground cinnamon to create the filling.

4. Shape Dough:

    - Punch down the risen dough to release the air. Divide it into golf ball-sized portions.
    - Flatten each ball in your hand, add a spoonful of the filling in the center, and then seal the edges, forming a round pancake.

5. Heat Oil:

    - Heat a skillet or pan over medium heat and add enough vegetable oil to coat the bottom.

6. Pan-Fry Hotteok:

    - Place the filled dough balls in the pan, seam side down. Press them gently with a spatula to flatten.
    - Cook each side until golden brown and crispy, about 2-3 minutes per side.

7. Serve:

    - Remove hotteok from the pan and let them cool slightly before serving.

8. Enjoy:

    - Enjoy these sweet and indulgent Hotteok pancakes, perfect for a delightful treat or snack!

Yakgwa (Honey Cookies)

Ingredients:

For the Dough:

- 2 cups all-purpose flour
- 1/4 cup sesame oil
- 1/4 cup water

For the Syrup:

- 1/2 cup honey
- 1/4 cup sugar
- 1/4 cup water
- 1 teaspoon soy sauce
- 1/2 teaspoon ginger, finely minced (optional)

Oil for Frying:

- Vegetable oil for deep-frying

Instructions:

1. Prepare the Dough:

- In a mixing bowl, combine all-purpose flour, sesame oil, and water. Knead the mixture until it forms a smooth dough. Cover and let it rest for about 30 minutes.

2. Roll and Cut:

- On a floured surface, roll out the dough to about 1/4-inch thickness. Cut the rolled-out dough into desired shapes, traditionally diamond-shaped or rectangles.

3. Make the Syrup:

- In a saucepan, combine honey, sugar, water, soy sauce, and minced ginger (if using). Heat the mixture over low heat, stirring continuously until the sugar dissolves and the syrup thickens slightly. Remove from heat and let it cool.

4. Fry the Cookies:

- In a deep fryer or a deep, heavy pot, heat vegetable oil to 350°F (175°C). Fry the cut dough pieces in batches until they puff up and turn golden brown.

5. Coat with Syrup:

- Once the cookies are fried, dip each one into the prepared honey syrup, ensuring they are well coated. Allow excess syrup to drip off.

6. Let it Set:

- Place the coated cookies on a wire rack or parchment paper to let the syrup set.

7. Enjoy:

- Once the honey cookies have cooled and the syrup has set, they are ready to be enjoyed. Yakgwa is often served during festive occasions and celebrations in Korean cuisine.

Chapssal Tteok (Glutinous Rice Cake)

Ingredients:

For Plain Chapssal Tteok:

- 2 cups sweet rice flour (chapssal-garu)
- 1 cup water
- Pinch of salt

For Filling (Optional):

- Sweet red bean paste (anko)
- Chopped nuts or seeds
- Honey or sugar

Instructions:

1. Prepare the Rice Cake Dough:

   - In a bowl, mix sweet rice flour (chapssal-garu), water, and a pinch of salt. Stir until you have a smooth batter.

2. Steam the Dough:

   - Pour the batter into a heatproof dish or a shallow pan suitable for steaming. Smooth the surface with a spatula. Steam over high heat for about 20-30 minutes or until the rice cake is fully cooked.

3. Check Doneness:

   - To check if the rice cake is done, insert a toothpick or skewer into the center. If it comes out clean, the rice cake is ready.

4. Shape the Rice Cake:

   - While the rice cake is still warm, knead it on a lightly oiled surface. Be cautious as it will be hot. You can wear food-safe gloves to protect your hands.

5. Divide and Fill (Optional):

- If you want to make filled rice cakes, divide the dough into small portions. Flatten each portion and add a spoonful of sweet red bean paste, chopped nuts, or a bit of honey or sugar in the center. Fold the edges over to seal the filling.

6. Shape and Serve:

- Shape the plain or filled rice cake portions into rounds or cylinders. Let them cool to room temperature.

7. Enjoy:

- Chapssal Tteok can be enjoyed on its own or with a dusting of sweet soybean flour (injeolmi) or coated in sesame seeds. It's a delightful and chewy treat commonly enjoyed in Korean cuisine.

Patbingsu (Red Bean Shaved Ice)

Ingredients:

For Shaved Ice:

- 4 cups shaved ice or finely crushed ice

For Red Bean Topping:

- 1 cup sweetened red bean paste (pat or adzuki bean paste)

For Milk Drizzle:

- 1/2 cup condensed milk or sweetened condensed milk

For Toppings:

- Fresh fruit slices (strawberries, mango, kiwi)
- Rice cakes (tteok)
- Nuts (almonds, peanuts)
- Cereal flakes
- Vanilla ice cream (optional)

Instructions:

1. Prepare Shaved Ice:

- If you don't have a shaved ice machine, you can crush ice in a blender until it reaches a snow-like consistency. Alternatively, you can buy pre-shaved ice.

2. Assemble Patbingsu:

- Place the shaved ice in a large bowl or serving dish.

3. Add Red Bean Topping:

- Spoon sweetened red bean paste over the shaved ice. You can adjust the amount according to your preference.

4. Drizzle with Milk:

- Generously drizzle condensed milk or sweetened condensed milk over the shaved ice and red bean paste. The amount can be adjusted based on your sweetness preference.

5. Add Toppings:

- Customize your patbingsu with various toppings. Add fresh fruit slices, rice cakes, nuts, cereal flakes, or even a scoop of vanilla ice cream.

6. Serve Immediately:

- Patbingsu is best enjoyed immediately before the shaved ice begins to melt.

7. Enjoy:

- Indulge in the refreshing and sweet flavors of Patbingsu, a popular Korean shaved ice dessert, especially delightful on a hot day!

Hoddeok (Korean Sweet Pancake)

Ingredients:

For Dough:

- 2 1/2 cups all-purpose flour
- 1 cup lukewarm milk
- 2 tablespoons sugar
- 2 tablespoons melted butter
- 1 teaspoon active dry yeast
- 1/2 teaspoon salt

For Filling:

- 1 cup brown sugar
- 1/2 cup chopped nuts (peanuts, walnuts)
- 1 teaspoon ground cinnamon

For Cooking:

- Vegetable oil for frying

Instructions:

1. Activate Yeast:

- In a bowl, combine lukewarm milk, sugar, and active dry yeast. Let it sit for about 5-10 minutes until the yeast activates and becomes frothy.

2. Make Dough:

- In a large mixing bowl, combine the activated yeast mixture, all-purpose flour, melted butter, and salt. Mix until a dough forms.

- Knead the dough on a floured surface for about 5-7 minutes until it becomes smooth and elastic. Place it back in the bowl, cover, and let it rise in a warm place for 1-2 hours or until it doubles in size.

3. Make Filling:

- In a separate bowl, mix brown sugar, chopped nuts, and ground cinnamon to create the filling.

4. Assemble Hoddeok:

- Punch down the risen dough and divide it into golf ball-sized portions. Flatten each ball and place a spoonful of the filling in the center. Gather the edges and seal to form a ball again.

5. Cook Hoddeok:

- Heat vegetable oil in a pan over medium heat. Place the filled dough balls in the pan, flatten them slightly with a spatula, and cook until both sides are golden brown.

6. Serve:

- Serve Hoddeok hot, allowing the melted sugar inside to create a gooey and delicious filling.

7. Enjoy:

- Enjoy these Korean sweet pancakes as a delightful and warm treat, perfect for cold days or as a sweet snack!

Injeolmi (Rice Cake Coated with Soybean Flour)

Ingredients:

For Rice Cake:

- 2 cups sweet rice (also known as glutinous rice or chapssal)
- 1 1/4 cups water
- 1/2 teaspoon salt

For Soybean Flour Coating:

- 1 cup sweet soybean flour (also known as injeolmi-garu)
- 1/4 teaspoon salt
- 2 tablespoons sugar (adjust to taste)

Instructions:

1. Prepare Rice Cake:

- Rinse the sweet rice under cold water until the water runs clear. Combine the rinsed sweet rice, water, and salt in a rice cooker or a pot. Cook the rice until it becomes soft and sticky.

2. Mash and Shape:

- While the rice is still warm, transfer it to a large mixing bowl. Mash the rice using a wooden spoon or a pestle until it becomes a smooth, sticky dough-like consistency.
- Wet your hands with water to prevent sticking. Shape the mashed rice into small bite-sized pieces or form it into rectangular blocks.

3. Coat with Soybean Flour:

- In a separate bowl, combine sweet soybean flour, salt, and sugar. Mix well.

- Roll each piece of shaped rice cake in the soybean flour mixture, ensuring it's fully coated. Shake off any excess flour.

4. Serve:

- Arrange the coated rice cakes on a plate or a serving tray.

5. Enjoy:

- Injeolmi is ready to be enjoyed! This traditional Korean rice cake is soft and chewy on the inside, with a delightful nutty flavor from the soybean flour coating. It's a popular snack or dessert in Korean cuisine.

Beverages:

Makgeolli (Traditional Rice Wine)

Ingredients:

For Making Rice Wine:

- 2 cups sweet rice (also known as glutinous rice or chapssal)
- 1/2 cup nuruk (fermentation starter)
- 4 cups water (for soaking rice)
- 4 cups water (for cooking rice)
- 2 cups nurungji (crust from the bottom of a pot after cooking rice)

For Sweetening (Optional):

- 1/2 cup sugar (adjust to taste)

Instructions:

1. Rinse and Soak Rice:

   - Rinse the sweet rice under cold water until the water runs clear. Soak the rice in 4 cups of water for at least 6 hours or overnight.

2. Cook Rice:

   - Drain the soaked rice and transfer it to a steamer. Steam the rice for about 30-40 minutes until it becomes soft and fully cooked.

3. Prepare Nurungji:

   - While the rice is still warm, let the crust (nurungji) form at the bottom of the pot. Gently scrape it off and set it aside.

4. Cool Rice:

- Allow the steamed rice to cool to room temperature.

5. Mix Nuruk:

   - In a large mixing bowl, crumble the nuruk into small pieces.

6. Combine Rice, Nuruk, and Nurungji:

   - Add the cooled steamed rice to the nuruk. Mix well to combine. Add the nurungji scraped from the pot and continue mixing.

7. Fermentation:

   - Transfer the rice mixture to a large fermentation jar or airtight container. Seal the container loosely to allow gases to escape during fermentation.
   - Store the container in a warm place for about 2-3 days, allowing the mixture to ferment. Stir the mixture once or twice a day.

8. Strain and Sweeten (Optional):

   - After fermentation, strain the liquid to separate the rice solids. Press down on the rice solids to extract as much liquid as possible.
   - If desired, sweeten the makgeolli by dissolving sugar in the liquid and stirring until it's fully dissolved. Adjust the sweetness to your liking.

9. Store:

   - Transfer the strained makgeolli to bottles or jars with lids. Seal the containers and refrigerate.

10. Serve:

    - Serve the chilled makgeolli in traditional bowls or cups. Shake or stir before serving to mix any settled sediment.

11. Enjoy:

- Enjoy this homemade makgeolli with its unique, slightly effervescent, and sweet flavor. It's a refreshing traditional Korean rice wine that's perfect for special occasions or casual gatherings.

Soju Cocktails

1. Soju Mojito:

Ingredients:

- 2 oz soju
- 1 oz fresh lime juice
- 1 teaspoon sugar
- Fresh mint leaves
- Soda water
- Ice cubes

Instructions:

Muddle fresh mint leaves and sugar in a glass.
Add soju and lime juice to the glass.
Fill the glass with ice cubes.
Top with soda water and stir gently.
Garnish with a mint sprig and a lime wheel.

2. Watermelon Soju Slush:

Ingredients:

- 2 cups fresh watermelon, cubed
- 2 oz soju
- 1 oz simple syrup
- Ice cubes

Instructions:

Blend watermelon cubes until smooth.
Strain the watermelon juice to remove pulp.
In a shaker, combine watermelon juice, soju, and simple syrup.
Shake well and pour over ice.
Garnish with watermelon slices.

3. Soju Sour:

Ingredients:

- 2 oz soju
- 3/4 oz simple syrup
- 1 oz fresh lemon juice
- Ice cubes

Instructions:

In a shaker, combine soju, simple syrup, and fresh lemon juice.
Shake well and strain into a glass over ice.
Garnish with a lemon wheel.

4. Cucumber Mint Soju Cooler:

Ingredients:

- 2 oz soju
- 1 oz cucumber juice
- 1/2 oz mint-infused simple syrup
- Soda water
- Fresh cucumber slices
- Mint leaves
- Ice cubes

Instructions:

In a shaker, combine soju, cucumber juice, and mint-infused simple syrup.
Shake well and strain into a glass filled with ice.
Top with soda water.
Garnish with cucumber slices and mint leaves.

5. Soju Sunrise:

Ingredients:

- 2 oz soju
- 3 oz orange juice
- 1/2 oz grenadine
- Orange slices
- Ice cubes

Instructions:

Fill a glass with ice cubes.
Pour soju and orange juice into the glass.
Slowly pour grenadine over the back of a spoon to create a layered effect.
Garnish with orange slices.

Feel free to adjust the ingredient quantities to suit your taste preferences!

Sikhye (Sweet Rice Drink)

Ingredients:

- 1 cup sweet rice (also known as glutinous rice or chapssal)
- 8 cups water
- 1 cup malt barley (yeotgireum)
- 1 cup sugar (adjust to taste)
- 1/4 teaspoon salt
- Pine nuts or jujube (for garnish, optional)

Instructions:

1. Rinse and Soak Sweet Rice:

- Rinse the sweet rice under cold water until the water runs clear. Soak the rice in water for about 2-3 hours.

2. Prepare Malt Barley:

- Rinse the malt barley under cold water. Set it aside.

3. Boil Sweet Rice:

- In a large pot, bring 8 cups of water to a boil. Drain the soaked sweet rice and add it to the boiling water. Cook over medium heat until the rice is fully cooked and the water turns cloudy.

4. Add Malt Barley:

- Add the malt barley to the pot with the cooked sweet rice. Stir well and let it simmer over low heat for about 20-30 minutes. This helps extract the enzymes from the malt.

5. Strain:

- Strain the liquid into a separate bowl, separating the rice and barley solids. Use a fine mesh strainer or cheesecloth to extract as much liquid as possible.

6. Sweeten:

- Add sugar to the strained liquid and stir until the sugar dissolves. Adjust the sweetness to your liking.

7. Cool and Ferment:

- Let the sweet rice drink cool to room temperature. Once cooled, cover the bowl with a cloth and let it ferment at room temperature for about 6-8 hours or overnight.

8. Serve:

- Serve the sikhye chilled. You can garnish it with pine nuts or jujube if desired.

9. Enjoy:

- Enjoy this traditional Korean sweet rice drink, sikhye, as a refreshing and mildly sweet beverage. It's often served as a dessert or during special occasions.

Bokbunja-ju (Black Raspberry Wine)

Ingredients:

- 1 pound fresh black raspberries (bokbunja)
- 2 cups soju or vodka
- 1 cup honey or sugar (adjust to taste)
- 1 cinnamon stick (optional)
- 1-2 slices of ginger (optional)

Instructions:

1. Prepare Black Raspberries:

- Wash the black raspberries thoroughly and remove any stems or impurities.

2. Combine Ingredients:

- In a clean glass jar or airtight container, combine the black raspberries, soju or vodka, honey or sugar, cinnamon stick (if using), and ginger slices (if using).

3. Seal and Shake:

- Seal the container tightly and shake it well to mix the ingredients.

4. Store in a Cool Place:

- Place the container in a cool, dark place for at least 3 weeks to allow the flavors to meld and the black raspberries to infuse into the alcohol.

5. Strain:

- After the infusion period, strain the liquid to remove the black raspberry solids. You can use a fine mesh strainer or cheesecloth for this process.

6. Bottle:

- Transfer the strained black raspberry wine into clean bottles. You can use a funnel to make the process easier.

7. Age (Optional):

    - Allow the wine to age for an additional few weeks to enhance the flavor. You can store it in the refrigerator or a cool place.

8. Serve:

    - Serve the Bokbunja-ju chilled. It can be enjoyed on its own or used in various cocktails.

9. Enjoy Responsibly:

    - Enjoy this homemade Black Raspberry Wine responsibly, either as a sipping drink or as a unique addition to cocktails.

Omija-cha (Five-Flavor Tea)

Ingredients:

- 1/4 cup dried omija berries (also known as Schisandra berries)
- 4 cups water
- Honey or sugar to taste
- Lemon slices (optional)
- Mint leaves (optional)

Instructions:

1. Rinse Omija Berries:

- Rinse the dried omija berries under cold water to remove any impurities.

2. Boil Water:

- In a pot, bring 4 cups of water to a boil.

3. Steep Omija Berries:

- Add the rinsed omija berries to the boiling water. Reduce the heat to low, cover, and let it simmer for about 15-20 minutes. This will allow the flavors of the omija berries to infuse into the water.

4. Strain:

- After simmering, strain the liquid to separate the omija berries from the tea. You can use a fine mesh strainer or cheesecloth for this process.

5. Sweeten (Optional):

- Add honey or sugar to the omija tea, adjusting the sweetness to your liking. Stir well until the sweetener dissolves.

6. Chill:

   - Allow the omija tea to cool to room temperature and then refrigerate it until it's chilled.

7. Serve:

   - Serve the omija-cha over ice. You can garnish it with lemon slices or mint leaves for added freshness and flavor.

8. Enjoy:

   - Enjoy this unique and refreshing Five-Flavor Tea, known for its complex taste profile. Omija-cha is believed to have five distinct flavors: sweet, sour, salty, bitter, and pungent. It's a popular traditional Korean tea with potential health benefits.

Yuja-cha (Citron Tea)

Ingredients:

- 3-4 large yuja (citron) fruits
- 1 cup sugar (adjust to taste)
- 4 cups water

Instructions:

1. Wash and Slice Yuja:

    - Wash the yuja fruits thoroughly. Slice them thinly, including the peel and seeds. Remove any seeds that are easily accessible.

2. Boil Water:

    - In a pot, bring 4 cups of water to a boil.

3. Simmer Yuja Slices:

    - Add the sliced yuja to the boiling water. Reduce the heat to low, cover, and let it simmer for about 15-20 minutes. This allows the yuja slices to soften and release their flavors.

4. Strain:

    - After simmering, strain the liquid to separate the yuja slices from the tea. You can use a fine mesh strainer or cheesecloth for this process.

5. Sweeten:

    - Add sugar to the yuja tea, adjusting the sweetness to your liking. Stir well until the sugar dissolves.

6. Store:

- Allow the yuja-cha to cool to room temperature. Once cooled, you can transfer it to a glass jar or bottle for storage.

7. Serve:

- Serve the yuja-cha by diluting it with hot or cold water, depending on your preference. Adjust the concentration to suit your taste.

8. Enjoy:

- Enjoy this soothing and fragrant Citron Tea. It's often served as a comforting beverage during cold weather, and some people also enjoy it with a spoonful of honey for added sweetness and health benefits.

Insam-cha (Ginseng Tea)

Ingredients:

- 2-3 slices of Korean red ginseng or 1 teaspoon of Korean red ginseng powder
- 1 cup water
- Honey or sweetener (optional)

Instructions:

1. Choose Ginseng:

- Select high-quality Korean red ginseng roots or ginseng powder for the best flavor and health benefits.

2. Prepare Ginseng:

- If using ginseng roots, wash them thoroughly and slice them thinly. If using ginseng powder, measure out the desired amount.

3. Boil Water:

- In a pot, bring 1 cup of water to a boil.

4. Steep Ginseng:

- Add the sliced ginseng or ginseng powder to the boiling water. Reduce the heat to low, cover, and let it simmer for about 15-20 minutes. This allows the ginseng to infuse into the water.

5. Strain (Optional):

- After simmering, you can strain the liquid to remove the ginseng pieces if you prefer a smoother tea. Use a fine mesh strainer or cheesecloth for this process.

6. Sweeten (Optional):

- If desired, add honey or a sweetener of your choice to the ginseng tea. Stir well until the sweetener is fully dissolved. Adjust the sweetness to your liking.

7. Serve:

- Serve the insam-cha hot. You can also let it cool and refrigerate it to enjoy as a cold beverage.

8. Enjoy:

- Enjoy this invigorating and earthy Ginseng Tea. Insam-cha is known for its potential health benefits, and it's often consumed for its adaptogenic properties and energy-boosting effects.

Saenggang-cha (Ginger Tea)

Ingredients:

- 1 cup fresh ginger, peeled and thinly sliced
- 4 cups water
- Honey or sweetener (optional)
- Lemon slices (optional)
- Fresh mint leaves (optional)

Instructions:

1. Prepare Ginger:

- Peel fresh ginger and slice it thinly. You can adjust the quantity of ginger based on your taste preferences.

2. Boil Water:

- In a pot, bring 4 cups of water to a boil.

3. Add Ginger:

- Add the sliced ginger to the boiling water. Reduce the heat to low, cover, and let it simmer for about 15-20 minutes. This allows the ginger to infuse into the water.

4. Strain (Optional):

- After simmering, you can strain the liquid to remove the ginger pieces if you prefer a smoother tea. Use a fine mesh strainer or cheesecloth for this process.

5. Sweeten (Optional):

- If desired, add honey or a sweetener of your choice to the ginger tea. Stir well until the sweetener is fully dissolved. Adjust the sweetness to your liking.

6. Add Lemon and Mint (Optional):

    - For added flavor, you can squeeze fresh lemon juice into the tea and garnish with lemon slices and mint leaves.

7. Serve:

    - Serve the saenggang-cha hot. You can also let it cool and refrigerate it to enjoy as a cold beverage.

8. Enjoy:

    - Enjoy this warming and flavorful Ginger Tea. Saenggang-cha is known for its potential health benefits, including its soothing effect on the digestive system and its ability to provide warmth during cold weather.

Baekseju (Herbal Rice Wine)

Ingredients:

For Herbal Mixture:

- 1 cup of various Korean medicinal herbs (such as ginseng, jujube, cinnamon, ginger, etc.)
- 2-3 tablespoons nuruk (fermentation starter)
- 1 cup rice wine (makgeolli) or water

For Rice Wine Base:

- 2 cups sweet rice (also known as glutinous rice or chapssal)
- 6 cups water

For Sweetening (Optional):

- Honey or sugar to taste

Instructions:

1. Prepare Medicinal Herbs:

- Gather a variety of Korean medicinal herbs. Common choices include ginseng, jujube, cinnamon, ginger, and more. You can find pre-packaged herbal mixtures specifically for making baekseju in some Korean grocery stores.

2. Make Rice Wine Base:

- Rinse sweet rice under cold water until the water runs clear. In a pot, combine the rinsed sweet rice with 6 cups of water. Cook the rice until it becomes soft and fully cooked.

3. Cool Rice Wine Base:

- Allow the rice wine base to cool to room temperature.

4. Make Herbal Mixture:

    - In a separate bowl, soak the medicinal herbs in 1 cup of rice wine or water for a few hours or overnight. This helps release the flavors of the herbs.

5. Blend Herbs:

    - After soaking, blend the herbs and rice wine mixture until it becomes a smooth paste.

6. Strain Herbal Paste:

    - Strain the herbal paste to separate the liquid from the solid particles. Use a fine mesh strainer or cheesecloth for this process.

7. Combine Rice Wine Base and Herbal Extract:

    - Combine the strained herbal extract with the cooled rice wine base. Mix well.

8. Add Nuruk:

    - Add 2-3 tablespoons of nuruk (fermentation starter) to the mixture. Stir to incorporate.

9. Fermentation:

    - Transfer the mixture to a fermentation jar or airtight container. Seal the container loosely to allow gases to escape during fermentation.
    - Allow the baekseju to ferment in a cool, dark place for about 2-3 weeks. Stir the mixture once a day during the fermentation period.

10. Strain and Bottle:

- After fermentation, strain the baekseju to remove any remaining solid particles. Bottle the liquid in clean containers.

11. Sweeten (Optional):

- If desired, sweeten the baekseju by adding honey or sugar to taste. Stir until the sweetener is fully dissolved.

12. Age (Optional):

- Allow the baekseju to age for a few more weeks to enhance the flavor. You can store it in the refrigerator or a cool place.

13. Serve:

- Serve the baekseju chilled. It can be enjoyed on its own or used in cocktails.

14. Enjoy Responsibly:

- Enjoy this homemade Herbal Rice Wine responsibly. Baekseju is known for its unique herbal flavor and potential health benefits.

www.ingramcontent.com/pod-product-compliance
Lightning Source LLC
LaVergne TN
LVHW081553060526
838201LV00054B/1885